HENSEL: STRING QUARTET IN E FLAT

The String Quartet in E flat major (1834) by Fanny Hensel, née Mendelssohn, is one of the most important works by a female composer written in the nineteenth century. Composed at a turning point in her life (as Hensel was not only grappling with her own creative voice but also coming to terms with her identity as a married woman and the role her family expected of her), the quartet is significant in showing a woman composing in a genre that was then almost exclusively the domain of male artists. Benedict Taylor's illuminating book situates itself within developing scholarly discourse on the music of women composers, going beyond apologetics – or condemnation of those who hindered their development – to examine the strength and qualities of the music and how it responded to the most progressive works of the period.

BENEDICT TAYLOR is Reader at the Reid School of Music, University of Edinburgh. Publications include *Mendelssohn, Time and Memory: The Romantic Conception of Cyclic Form* (2011), *The Melody of Time: Music and Temporality in the Romantic Era* (2016), and *Music, Subjectivity, and Schumann* (2022).

T0334706

NEW CAMBRIDGE MUSIC HANDBOOKS

Series Editor

NICOLE GRIMES, UNIVERSITY OF CALIFORNIA, IRVINE

The New Cambridge Music Handbooks series provides accessible introductions to landmarks in music history, written by leading experts in their field. Encompassing a wide range of musical styles and genres, it embraces the music of hitherto-under-represented creators as well as re-imagining works from the established canon. It will enrich the musical experience of students, scholars, listeners and performers alike.

Books in the Series

Hensel: String Quartet in E flat
Benedict Taylor

Berlioz: *Symphonie Fantastique*
Julian Rushton

Margaret Bonds: The Montgomery Variations and Du Bois 'Credo'
John Michael Cooper

Robert Schumann: Piano Concerto
Julian Horton

Schoenberg: 'Night Music', *Verklärte Nacht* and *Erwartung*
Arnold Whittall

Forthcoming Titles

Schubert: The 'Great' Symphony in C major
Suzannah Clark

Bach: The Cello Suites
Edward Klorman

Clara Schumann: Piano Concerto in A minor Op. 7
Julie Pedneault-Deslauriers

Donizetti: *Lucia di Lammermoor*
Mark Pottinger

Beethoven: String Quartet Op. 130
Elaine Sisman

Louise Farrenc: Nonet for Winds and Strings
Marie Sumner Lott

Cavalleria rusticana and *Pagliacci*
Alexandra Wilson

HENSEL: STRING QUARTET IN E FLAT

BENEDICT TAYLOR

University of Edinburgh

CAMBRIDGE
UNIVERSITY PRESS

CAMBRIDGE
UNIVERSITY PRESS

Shaftesbury Road, Cambridge CB2 8EA, United Kingdom

One Liberty Plaza, 20th Floor, New York, NY 10006, USA

477 Williamstown Road, Port Melbourne, VIC 3207, Australia

314–321, 3rd Floor, Plot 3, Splendor Forum, Jasola District Centre, New Delhi – 110025, India

103 Penang Road, #05–06/07, Visioncrest Commercial, Singapore 238467

Cambridge University Press is part of Cambridge University Press & Assessment, a department of the University of Cambridge.

We share the University's mission to contribute to society through the pursuit of education, learning and research at the highest international levels of excellence.

www.cambridge.org
Information on this title: www.cambridge.org/9781316513842

DOI: 10.1017/9781009076159

First published 2024

A catalogue record for this publication is available from the British Library.

A Cataloging-in-Publication data record for this book is available from the Library of Congress

ISBN 978-1-316-51384-2 Hardback
ISBN 978-1-009-07489-6 Paperback

CONTENTS

Contents

FIGURES

TABLES

MUSICAL EXAMPLES

PREFACE

I must first thank Nicole Grimes, the ever-supportive series editor for the New Cambridge Music Handbooks, for originally asking me to contribute a volume to the relaunched series, and for her patience while I slipped first from discussing Clara Schumann to Fanny Hensel and then vacillated as to the extent of my coverage of her chamber music. Angela Mace has similarly been a constant and generous source of encouragement in all matters Henselian, while conversations with Thomas Schmidt also contributed valuable ideas. To Julian Horton and Steven Vande Moortele I owe a stimulating discussion of the outer movements of the 'Easter' Sonata, which has helped inform and clarify my thoughts on that work. Andrew Jennings, Norman Fischer, and Vicki Sirota all graciously helped clear up details of the 1982 premiere in New York and the events leading up to this. The book was written while on sabbatical in the autumn of 2021, part of which was spent at the Hochschule für Musik und Theater Hamburg, and I would like to thank the Alexander von Humboldt Stiftung for a renewal of my research stay as a Humboldtian, as well as Jan Philipp Sprick for acting as host. My ideas on the quartet were presented in a seminar in November 2021, and I likewise extend my thanks to Jan Philipp, Oliver Mathes, and Lujia Sun for their insightful contributions and thoughts on the piece. One thing that became clear from our discussion was the richness of Hensel's music, and how there is still so much to explore, even in this particular piece. Parts of this book were also presented at a colloquium at the Faculty of Music at Oxford in March 2022, and I would similarly like to thank the attentive audience for their helpful questions and comments.

Musical examples in this volume have been prepared from the autograph of Hensel's quartet found in the Staatsbibliothek Berlin and available online (https://digital.staatsbibliothek-berlin.de/wer

kansicht/?PPN=PPN1724626299). Only a handful of Hensel's works were published in her lifetime and the immediately following years, and for designation purposes scholars typically use the numbers provided by the thematic catalogue made by Renate Hellwig-Unruh (H-U) instead of opus numbers (Renate Hellwig-Unruh, *Fanny Hensel geb. Mendelssohn Bartholdy: Thematisches Verzeichnis der Kompositionen* (Adliswil: Edition Kunzelmann, 2000)). In cases where no opus number (or a highly misleading posthumous one) for her brother Felix Mendelssohn's music is available, I similarly use MWV numbers from the recent thematic catalogue by Ralf Wehner (*Felix Mendelssohn Bartholdy: Thematisch-systematisches Verzeichnis der musikalischen Werke* (Wiesbaden: Breitkopf und Härtel, 2009)).

A word on naming conventions may also be useful. Although born Fanny Cäcilia Mendelssohn, and adopting the additional family name Bartholdy on baptism in 1816, from her marriage in 1829 until her death in 1847 the composer went under the name of Fanny Hensel ('F. Hensel' is written on the autograph title page of the quartet, and in publications she named herself 'Fanny Hensel, b. Mendelssohn-Bartholdy'). In order to distinguish between her and her famous younger brother Felix Mendelssohn, I generally adopt the surnames Hensel and Mendelssohn respectively, even if occasionally referring back to the time before marriage. Still, when referring to the child or teenager, I am often happy to call her simply Fanny, which avoids the mild anachronism (as well as the potential confusion in places with her future husband, Wilhelm Hensel) and emphasises the close-knit family environment with her brother Felix. After 1829, however, I try to minimise familiar first-name reference to both, a practice which, while not uncommon in recent literature, may appear condescending to both figures.

INTRODUCTION

The String Quartet in E flat major (H-U277, 1834) is a pivotal work in the musical output of Fanny Hensel, née Mendelssohn (1805–47). One of her most ambitious and individual compositions, the quartet was written at a turning point in Hensel's life, in which she was not only grappling with her own creative voice and future musical direction but coming to terms with her identity as a married woman and the role society and her family expected of her. The quartet's origins go back to an unfinished piano sonata written in the autumn of 1829, a momentous year for Hensel, in which the then-twenty-three-year-old's idolised younger brother and closest musical confidant, Felix Mendelssohn (1809–47), had left the family home in Berlin for several years of travel, and she married her long-standing fiancé Wilhelm Hensel, with whom she would live for the remaining eighteen years of her life. 'This year will mark an important chapter in our family life', she writes dramatically in the first entry of a new diary, started on 4 January that year: 'Felix, our soul, is leaving; the beginning of the second part of my life stands before me . . . everything stirs and moves around us.'[1] Just as 1829 formed a crossroads in her private life, so too the quartet marks a crossroads in her creative endeavours. Already an experienced composer, Hensel's métier had nevertheless been in the small-scale genres of the lied and piano piece. Composing a string quartet was a major statement of ambition at this time, and in refashioning material into a quartet in 1834, Hensel was staking out a path in an elite genre associated with the highest and most exacting compositional standards. It was also one that – unlike the piano miniature or song – was almost exclusively the domain of male composers. As commentators have noted, this is one of the first string quartets ever written by a woman, and in taking this step Hensel was venturing into more or less unprecedented territory.[2]

Introduction

Alongside her later D minor Piano Trio (1847) and the two mature piano sonatas – the 'Easter' Sonata (H-U235, 1828) and G minor Sonata (H-U395, 1843) – the E flat Quartet is the most significant composition Hensel would complete in a canonic classical instrumental genre. Unlike the piano trio, which was published posthumously in 1850 as Hensel's Op. 11, the quartet did not see the light of day until the 1980s. Its own reception history is thus short and confined to the modern age. Yet rather than presenting an awkward challenge to scholarly inquiry, this dearth of critical reception offers the present-day scholar and listener the freedom to concentrate on the actual qualities of the music, unencumbered by long-standing issues of reception that have accompanied many women composers from an earlier period. And equally, the quartet itself provides an intriguing and virtually unparalleled instance of practical reception history (*Wirkungsgeschichte*, to give the useful German term). The quartet documents Hensel's interaction with the music of her brother – music for both of them formed an intimate means of correspondence – and the two siblings' mutual creative responses to the recent late works of Beethoven, at this time barely known outside small circles of enthusiasts.[3] Rather than showing a composer awed by the 'shadow of Beethoven' (as later, post-1850 polemics would suggest), the quartet instead reveals a highly assured technique and an unselfconscious creative engagement with the most modern compositional developments of the time, which Hensel takes up and transforms into something quite her own. The quartet allows us a glimpse into a private realm of compositional reception that has remained hidden for over a century and a half.

Finally, this quartet was also the subject of an important critical exchange with her younger brother carried out by correspondence over the winter of 1834–5 that is not only highly revealing as to their respective musical and aesthetic proclivities, but arguably affected – for better or for worse – the direction of Hensel's subsequent compositional development. Felix Mendelssohn's criticism of his elder sister's work constitutes one of the most extensive testimonies on matters of form and aesthetics from this usually reticent musical commentator and highlights important features of Hensel's music just as it reveals the strong differences that were emerging between the two siblings. Regrettably, Mendelssohn may have been partly responsible for putting his sister off from pursuing further essays in large-scale instrumental forms in the following years and discouraging the experimental paths opened up by the quartet. Yet Hensel ultimately came to terms with the criticism, and her later development as a composer negotiated these conflicting tendencies in a way that still remains very much her own.

Hensel and Current Research

Since the original series of Cambridge Music Handbooks (1991–2001), the study of the music of women composers has advanced dramatically. None of the first thirty-eight volumes was devoted to a work by a female composer. Now two decades on, with the relaunch of the series, there is welcome opportunity to redress this situation by examining a major work from a figure who not only counts as one of the most important women composers of the nineteenth century but indeed as one of the most talented composers of any era. In doing so, I would contend, we have also reached a stage within the developing scholarly discourse on the music of women composers that goes well beyond either apologetics or condemnation of those who hindered their development, in which we are free to examine the qualities of the music in detail and how it responded to and stands side by-side with the most original works of the time.[4]

Detailed study of Hensel's music is still comparatively thin on the ground, though it has unquestionably picked up in recent years. In a pioneering article on Hensel's songs from 2011, Stephen Rodgers observed that 'the bulk of research on Fanny Mendelssohn Hensel to date has focused primarily on either the historical or editorial; analysis of her music, however, is rare'.[5] To be fair, there had been a modest number of analytical accounts of Hensel's music appearing in German scholarship since the late 1990s, but the observation was undoubtedly true of English-language writing at the time.[6] In the decade since then, substantial strides have been made towards deepening our understanding of

3

Hensel's music, most notably by Rodgers himself in several important articles and a 2021 edited volume on her songs.[7] However, these accounts are almost entirely confined to Hensel's songs and piano music, which, while central to her musical activities, are nevertheless only part of her remarkable output. More still has to be done in order to appreciate, in Rodgers's words, 'the full scope of Hensel's achievement as a composer'.[8]

Why the String Quartet then? There are, naturally, other pieces that might equally have been chosen for a first Cambridge Music Handbook on Hensel's music. The D minor Piano Trio is the quartet's main rival in the realm of chamber music, and, having been published soon after Hensel's death, has received more extensive exposure; to this day it is probably programmed more regularly. Yet the earlier quartet is in many ways an even more individual work, fascinating for what it shows us about Hensel's own compositional development at a crucial formative period in her life. Her piano cycle *Das Jahr* (1841), meanwhile, would also have a strong claim to constituting Hensel's masterpiece and has plenty of advocates: Hensel's biographer, R. Larry Todd, for instance, holds it to be 'arguably her most impressive accomplishment'.[9] On the other hand, *Das Jahr* has already received ample attention in a number of articles, whereas the quartet has hardly been considered in English-language scholarship.[10] Moreover, the quartet is also noteworthy in showing a woman composing in a genre then held to be the preserve of male artists; the more intimate, 'feminine' sphere of short piano pieces and song was considered suitable for women composers, rather than chamber music for strings. Indeed, this highlights one of the dilemmas encountered making any selection from Hensel's compositional oeuvre, one that is worth briefly addressing here before embarking upon the remainder of the study.

Genre, Gender, and the Question of Choice

Recent decades have seen keen interest in the relationship between musical genres and gender, so much so that it is more or less a truism today that certain genres are marked with respect to gender: large-scale, public works or those in learned genres such as the symphony or string quartet are strongly associated with the masculine sphere, in contrast to the feminine connotations of domestic genres such as the lied or piano miniature.[11] A series of handbooks dedicated to major works or 'masterpieces', however, almost invariably gravitates towards large-scale, monumental works at the expense of smaller pieces, even if the latter make up a more significant part of a given composer's oeuvre. A string quartet, concerto, or symphony makes a more obvious focal point for a study than a set of songs or small-scale piano pieces (at a stretch, a song cycle might be included). There is, in other words, a likely predisposition to privilege genres perceived as 'masculine' over 'feminine' ones in selecting a suitable magnum opus. This tension is merely exacerbated when it comes to the output of a female composer such as Hensel, most of whose output, published and unpublished, consists of songs and piano pieces. The implication here is that if one selects a large-scale instrumental work by a woman, one is liable to reinscribe the (purportedly masculinist) 'great works' model that implicitly devalues smaller creations as insignificant; yet in focussing on small-scale works in intimate genres often typecast as feminine, one nevertheless restricts a female composer to gendered expectations.

While it is necessary to acknowledge this concern, we should nevertheless not overstate the issue: the problem is not insurmountable, in that both smaller and larger genres can and ideally should be examined. In this sense, the present account of the String Quartet is intended to complement the already quite extensive recent analytical coverage given to Hensel's songs and piano music. Neither should such binaries be exaggerated: even if genres such as the symphony or string quartet were less accessible for a woman composing at this historical juncture, one need not perpetuate the reductive assumption that there is something inherently or necessarily masculine about them. While Hensel may have taken on some of this ideology, the social constraints she experienced as a woman at that time should not be conflated with essential traits of either gender or genre. And chamber music,

5

above all, constitutes a particularly fertile repertory for negotiating these questions.

As recent work has shown, the neat separation between a male public sphere and female private sphere in the nineteenth century breaks down when it comes to chamber music, which, as Marie Sumner Lott argues, 'complicates the convenient binaries used by modern scholars to understand the Romantic era'. Though largely private or semi-private, in this period 'string chamber music was largely a male-exclusive activity', she holds.[12] Where Hensel is especially interesting in this respect is in how she engaged with this 'masculine' discursive practice of the string quartet from within her 'feminine', domestic sphere of music-making. In this context, it is worth recalling a point made earlier by Michael Steinberg, who has argued that the musical activities of the Mendelssohn household formed an intriguing conjunction between male and female worlds. Speaking of Hensel's celebrated brother, he claims:

> Within his professional circles and his family, Felix was a fairly typical male . . . Yet the musical culture he absorbed from his family was transmitted through the work and talent of important women, especially his great-aunt, Sara Levy, as well as his sister [Fanny Hensel]. [Thus] when Felix exercised his male priority to take his music into the public sphere – an option denied Fanny – he translated a domestic, and in a specific sense a female, discourse into a public and male one.

Fanny, on the other hand, remained within the intimate family sphere; but in works like the String Quartet we might conversely witness her translating a male discourse into her female environment. All this lends support to Steinberg's assertion that 'music in the [Mendelssohn] family sphere meant the promise of cultural dialogue' – a dialogue that is also, by implication, between gendered spheres of activity, musical genre, and social mores.[13]

These questions of gender and genre will run throughout the following account; but we should also remember that both art and history are rarely simple enough to be reduced to binary oppositions, and have an ability to confound, complicate, and renegotiate typecasting. Of few other figures is this more true than of Fanny Hensel.

Notes

1. Fanny Hensel, diary entry for 4 January 1829, in *Fanny Hensel: Tagebücher*, ed. Hans-Günter Klein and Rudolf Elvers (Wiesbaden: Breitkopf & Härtel, 2002), p. 1.

2. Maddelena Laura Lombardini Sirmen, a Venetian pupil of Tartini, had published six quartets back in 1769; it seems unlikely Hensel would have known of them, however.

3. This idea of music as private correspondence is developed by Cornelia Bartsch in *Fanny Hensel, geb. Mendelssohn: Musik als Korrespondenz* (Kassel: Furore 2007).

4. An early impulse in this direction within Hensel studies was given by Marian Wilson Kimber, 'The "Suppression" of Fanny Mendelssohn: Rethinking Feminist Biography', *19th-Century Music*, 26/2 (2002), 113–29.

5. Stephen Rodgers, 'Fanny Hensel's Lied Aesthetic', *Journal of Musicological Research*, 30 (2011), 175–201 at p. 175. Honourable exceptions to this include earlier accounts of Hensel's piano music by Camilla Cai, Susan Wollenberg, and Marian Wilson Kimber.

6. See, for instance, chapters in Martina Helmig (ed.), *Fanny Hensel, geb. Mendelssohn Bartholdy: Das Werk* (Munich: edition text+kritik, 1997) and Beatrix Borchard and Monika Schwarz-Danuser (eds.), *Fanny Hensel geb. Mendelssohn Bartholdy: Komponieren zwischen Geselligskeitsideal und romantischer Musikästhetik* (Stuttgart: J. B. Metzler, 1999).

7. Stephen Rodgers (ed.), *The Songs of Fanny Hensel* (New York: Oxford University Press, 2021). See also Yonatan Malin, 'Hensel: Lyrical Expansions, Elisions, and Rhythmic Flow', in *Songs in Motion: Rhythm and Meter in the German Lied* (New York: Oxford University Press, 2010), pp. 69–94; Samuel Ng, 'Rotation as Metaphor: Fanny Hensel's Formal and Tonal Logic Reconsidered', *Indiana Theory Review*, 29/2 (2011), 31–70; Rodgers, 'Thinking (and Singing) in Threes: Triple Hypermeter and the Songs of Fanny Hensel', *Music Theory Online*, 17/1 (2011), and 'Fanny Hensel's Schematic Fantasies: or, The Art of Beginning', in Laurel Parsons and Brenda Ravenscroft (eds.), *Analytical Essays on Music by Women Composers* (New York: Oxford University Press, 2018), pp. 151–74; and Stephen Rodgers and Tyler Osborne, 'Prolongational Closure in the Lieder of Fanny Hensel', *Music Theory Online*, 26/3 (2020).

8. Stephen Rodgers, 'Introduction', *The Songs of Fanny Hensel*, p. 2.

9. R. Larry Todd, *Fanny Hensel: The Other Mendelssohn* (New York: Oxford University Press, 2010), p. 275.

10. On *Das Jahr*, see especially the fine account by Marian Wilson Kimber, 'Fanny Hensel's Seasons of Life: Poetic Epigrams, Vignettes, and

Meaning in *Das Jahr'*, *Journal of Musicological Research*, 27 (2008), 359–95, as well as John E. Toews, 'Memory and Gender in the Remaking of Fanny Mendelssohn's Musical Identity: The Chorale in *Das Jahr'*, *Musical Quarterly*, 77 (1993), 727–48, Sarah Rothenberg, '"Thus Far, but No Farther": Fanny Mendelssohn-Hensel's Unfinished Journey', *Musical Quarterly*, 77 (1993), 689–708, and R. Larry Todd, 'Issues of Stylistic Identity in Fanny Hensel's *Das Jahr* (1841)', in *Mendelssohn Essays* (New York: Routledge, 2008), pp. 249–60, as well as accounts in German by Annette Nubbemeyer, 'Italienerinnerungen im Klavieroeuvre Fanny Hensels: Das verschwiegene Programm im Klavierzyklus "Das Jahr"', in Helmig (ed.), *Fanny Hensel*, pp. 68–80, and Christian Thorau, 'Das spielende Bild des Jahres: Fanny Hensels Klavierzyklus *Das Jahr'*, in Borchard and Schwarz-Danuser (eds.), *Fanny Hensel*, pp. 73–89.

The two most useful English-language accounts of the String Quartet are found in larger surveys of Hensel's life and work: Todd's *Fanny Hensel*, pp. 179–86, and Angela R. Mace, 'Fanny Hensel, Felix Mendelssohn Bartholdy, and the Formation of the Mendelssohnian Style', PhD diss., Duke University, 2013, pp. 193–213. A brief but perceptive outline is given in Victoria Sirota's pioneering doctoral thesis 'The Life and Works of Fanny Mendelssohn Hensel', DMA diss., Boston University, 1981, pp. 239–44. Analyses of the quartet's finale and first movements are also offered by Frances Shi Hui Lee, 'Unconventional: Sonata-Form Manipulations in the Multi-Movement Works of Fanny Hensel', DMA diss., Rice University, 2020, pp. 71–90, and Catrina S. Kim, 'Formal Excess in the Opening Movement of Fanny Hensel's String Quartet in E flat Major (1834)', forthcoming in *Music Theory Spectrum*.

11. See for instance Marcia J. Citron, *Gender and the Musical Canon* (Cambridge: Cambridge University Press, 1993), Jeffrey Kallberg, *Chopin at the Boundaries: Sex, History, and Musical Genre* (Cambridge, MA: Harvard University Press, 1996), and with specific reference to Hensel, Matthew Head, 'Genre, Romanticism and Female Authorship: Fanny Hensel's "Scottish" Sonata in G Minor (1843)', *Nineteenth-Century Music Review*, 4/2 (2007), 67–88.

12. Marie Sumner Lott, *The Social Worlds of Nineteenth-Century Chamber Music* (Urbana: University of Illinois Press, 2015), pp. 18, 7.

13. Michael P. Steinberg, 'Introduction: Culture, Gender, and Music: A Forum on the Mendelssohn Family', *Musical Quarterly*, 77 (1993), 648–50 at 649.

2

BACKGROUND

Hensel's Musical Upbringing

Fanny Hensel was seemingly destined for music, being blessed with 'Bach fugal fingers' (so her mother claimed) following her arrival into the world on 14 November 1805. The eldest of four children (Felix, Rebecka, and Paul would follow in the next seven years), Fanny was born into a cultured and well-off family of assimilated German Jews. Her mother Lea, née Salomon, was remarkably well read and an accomplished pianist with a fondness for J. S. Bach, while her father Abraham was the son of the Enlightenment philosopher Moses Mendelssohn and had risen from modest beginnings to become a successful banker. In 1811, as a result of the French occupation, the family moved from Hamburg to Berlin, where apart from brief sojourns elsewhere Hensel would spend the rest of her life.

Not much is known in detail about Fanny's earliest musical education.[1] Alongside her brother Felix, she took piano lessons from Marie Bigot in Paris, Ludwig Berger in Berlin, and later in the 1820s briefly from Ignaz Moscheles. She evidently knew how to put her natural endowment to good use, as by the age of thirteen she was performing the preludes of Bach's *Well-Tempered Clavier* from memory. That same year, the eldest two siblings began theory and composition lessons with Carl Friedrich Zelter, a stickler for the Berlin Bach tradition and friend and musical correspondent of the grand old man of German letters, Johann Wolfgang von Goethe. By chance, one of Felix's exercise books from this period survives, which provides insight into the training he received from Zelter. It charts a rigorous course in thoroughbass and counterpoint up to three-part fugal writing.[2] We do not know for sure whether Fanny received identical instruction, but by 1819 she was composing songs and gavottes and was soon writing fugues alongside her younger brother. In December of that year, both Fanny and Felix penned songs as presents for their father's birthday, which are possibly the earliest surviving compositions of each.[3]

On 4 March 1820, Fanny started preserving her compositions in a musical album; Felix would do the same just three days later.[4] However, their compositional development was not to continue in parallel fashion. Soon after, in July of that year, Abraham wrote a letter to his eldest child on the occasion of her confirmation that has become well-nigh infamous in Hensel scholarship. A profession in music, her father wrote, could perhaps be considered for Felix, but for Fanny, as a young woman, music 'can and must only be an ornament'.[5] From this point on, her younger brother was able to expand out into larger, more 'public' genres: *Singspiele* (operas with dialogue), symphonies for string orchestra, concertos for violin and piano, and the like, which were often performed at the fortnightly *Sonntags Übungen* (Sunday Practices) at the family home in Berlin. Fanny, however, by all accounts equally talented and the elder by over three years, would continue her compositional efforts in domestic genres more suitable for a young lady, foremost among which were songs and piano pieces. Nevertheless, larger forms and chamber music were not inaccessible to her. Several larger-scale works from Hensel's teenage years exist, including a sonata movement in E major (H-U44, 1822), a Piano Quartet in A flat (H-U55, 1822), and a Piano Sonata in C minor (H-U128, 1824). What is noticeable even in these early works is how free Hensel's treatment of form is. Prophetic of her later music is the continual variation made of the opening material, use of contrapuntal techniques, and an expansive harmonic language that often ranges far from expected tonal centres.

Fanny, Felix, and a Shared Mendelssohnian Style?

If the limitations imposed by her environment made it hard for Fanny to keep up with her brother in all genres, she nevertheless found some outlet for any frustrated compositional ambitions in her role as advisor, critic, and closest musical confidant to Felix. 'Up to the present moment', she noted in 1822, 'I have watched the progress of his talent step by step and may say I have contributed to his development. I have always been his only musical adviser, and he never writes down a thought before submitting it to my judgement.'[6] The sixteen-year-old may be mildly overstating her case, perhaps stemming from a need for self-reassurance given her own limited opportunities for development, but there is no doubt that Felix had enormous respect for his sister's musical abilities. And although Fanny clearly looked up to her talented younger brother and, as with her whole family, would come more or less to idolise him, the musical interaction was not just one-way.

From the accounts left, it appears that the two siblings shared a remarkably close musical bond. Musical ideas passed from one to the other, advice and criticism were offered, enthusiasms were shared. As Angela Mace writes, 'the compositional proximity of the two composers in the 1820s was incredibly intimate; hardly a note was thought of or written down without the involvement of the other composer ... they critiqued their own music and the music of each other ... they worked through their compositional models together'.[7] In numerous cases, the two can be seen responding to each other in their musical compositions, reworking or answering the other's themes. Thus Fanny's C minor Piano Sonata, composed 'for Felix in his absence' as she wrote at the end of the manuscript, appears to rework the opening motive of her brother's own earlier G minor Piano Sonata (1821, Op. 105/MWV U30).[8] Later works are no less allusive; the String Quartet, as we will see, is full of such internal references. And though Felix's influence on Hensel 'was powerful, and often dominant', as Todd remarks, there is 'evidence of a two-sided compositional exchange between the two'.[9] Camilla Cai, for instance, has pointed to the likelihood that Mendelssohn's *Song without Words*, Op. 38 No. 5 (1837), took its bearings from one of Hensel's own *Songs for Pianoforte* written shortly before.[10] In some cases, it is unclear which piece came first. Even later in life, after adulthood and marriage took them on diverging paths, the connection remained. 'Isn't it peculiar how musical ideas sometimes seem to fly about in the air, and land here and there?' wrote Mendelssohn to his sister in 1837 on discovering that they had independently come up with almost identical themes. 'It's simply too funny – and it's lovely that our ideas remain so close.'[11]

Beyond these cases of shared material, their upbringing alongside each other resulted in close similarities in their musical style – so much so that a small number of Hensel's songs were able to be passed off under her brother's name. Mendelssohn's first two sets of songs, Opp. 8 and 9, each contain three songs by Hensel among their twelve numbers, which for a long time were believed by all but close acquaintances to be by Mendelssohn himself. A few decades back, some critics were prone to deplore this authorial subterfuge as demonstrating a male composer appropriating his sister's work. As their correspondence shows, however, Hensel was fully aware of this decision, and even had the leading role in the preparation of the Op. 9 set.[12] When Mendelssohn, short of time and pressed by his publisher, came to prepare the songs in 1829, he asked his sister to select as she saw fit, 'from my or her things', which she duly did, and throughout his life he readily admitted her authorship in private company (most famously to Queen Victoria, who had selected one of Hensel's songs, 'Italien', Op. 8 No. 3, as her favourite among his songs). Although not conforming to modern views on gender roles, this example constitutes an oblique response to the impediment to publishing resulting from Hensel's sex and social position at that time, one rooted in the musical kinship between the two and Mendelssohn's high regard for his sister's creations.[13]

Indeed, the idea of a 'common Mendelssohnian style' shared by the two siblings has often been raised. Some commentators are understandably hesitant to use the term, partly owing to the fact that this has often effectively meant treating Hensel as a copy of her more famous brother (with the problematic assumed dependency of the female on the male figure), and partly because this overlooks real differences in their musical output. Yet there is some justification for the idea, when properly qualified. First, we should note that more discerning observers had long recognised how Fanny, the elder by over three years, is at least as likely to have influenced Felix as vice versa. Their Danish contemporary, Niels Gade, implies this, writing in 1843 of the 'invention, skill, genius, and energy' of Hensel's music, which he had come to know from hearing her private performances at home in Berlin. 'They say that she exercised much influence on Felix Mendelssohn's musical development', he continues. 'She is namely older than he. Their compositions are very similar.'[14] Secondly, there are sufficient similarities between the two to warrant the label: it would be hard to think of any other pair of composers in the nineteenth century who can sound so alike. Where Hensel and Mendelssohn are most akin is in specific turns of phrase and their melodic material, which can be similar to a degree that almost confounds differentiation. Yet despite their common training and comparable technical command, in the way the two treat their material – most specifically in harmonic language and formal design – the two siblings are actually quite distinct, and on closer analysis could rarely be confused with each other.

Such differences were spotted even in their lifetimes, following Hensel's belated decision to publish her music under her own name, when a critic reviewing her *Lieder für Klavier* Op. 2 in 1847 contrasted the 'highly precise' manner of expression and economy of means in Mendelssohn's *Songs without Words* with Hensel's 'more complicated' expression in her own wordless *Songs*, in which 'fantasy is permitted a freer rein' and greater variety and breadth is sought.[15] In this sense, it might be helpful to read, as Mace suggests, a common 'Mendelssohnian style' coalescing over the 1820s while the two grew up together, which became increasingly differentiated after 1829 as they went their separate ways.[16]

Intimate Correspondences within the Family Circle

With music providing such an intimate bond between the siblings, there arose a remarkable potential for interacting through this medium. One of the most intriguing aspects of the Mendelssohn family practice is the idea that music formed a means of intimate, almost private communication between figures within the close circle, to an extent that complemented or perhaps even went beyond verbal language. In a famous remark Felix Mendelssohn would later make in a letter of 1842, he claims that music is a more precise form of communication than words. Whereas words can be ambiguous and liable to be misunderstood, 'what the music that I love expresses to me are not thoughts too unclear for words, but rather those too definite'.[17]

Thomas Schmidt has profitably related Mendelssohn's position to the theories of language promulgated by Johann Gottfried Herder and Wilhelm von Humboldt (a visitor to the Mendelssohn household in the 1820s), which understand language as a natural expression of the particular community from which it evolves: the smaller and closer-knit the community, the more subtle and nuanced the expression, though harder for outsiders to comprehend. For Mendelssohn, music was evidently like a language, one which in some cases could be more definite in its expression than general words (note that he does not claim all music possesses this precision, only 'the music that I love', 'good music'). The latter would obtain when dealing with like-minded people, especially those with whom, like his sister, he had grown up and shared such close musical ties, and who thus made his ideal listeners.[18] Cornelia Bartsch has subsequently developed this point in relation to the use of music as an intimate language between the Mendelssohn siblings and those in their immediate circle – the idea of 'music as correspondence'. Mendelssohn and Hensel's shared upbringing ensured music formed a private means of communication between them: they could address and respond to each other in their music sure of mutual understanding, in ways that those outside the close circle could often not 'get'.[19]

An important upshot of this belief is that taking music out of the private family environment and transferring it into the public sphere (as would occur with publication or public performance) was thereby removing it from its native environment and richest source of meaning and could make it open to misunderstanding or incomprehension. Here, the asymmetrical career paths of the two eldest siblings point to a division between two aesthetic and communicative spheres, one in which Hensel's limited situation was, curiously, not as great a drawback as it might at first appear. In choosing a profession in music, Bartsch holds, Mendelssohn faced a potential conflict in bringing the 'inward sources' of intimate musical communication out into the public gaze, one which his sister, discouraged from entering the public sphere, did not face until the end of her life when she chose to start publishing her music.[20] Mendelssohn, urged on by his father's demand to be a model of civic virtue, was acutely aware of the need for maintaining a professional profile, but just as aware that this would sometimes mean bringing to the public well-crafted and accessible works that lacked (for him) the meaning of his more personal creations. Conversely, he would never attempt to publish certain private works, such as the unassuming mini-opera *Die Heimkehr aus der Fremde* composed for his parents' silver anniversary in 1829, even though he would relate to a friend that it was the best thing he had written: the *Liederspiel* was too personal, too bound up with the meanings and private jokes of the close family circle for others to understand. Hensel's restriction to private forms of music-making thus kept her within the intimate realm that was the wellspring of the Mendelssohns' creativity; it also means that the full range of allusion and signification within her music might not be straightforward for us to uncover now as outsiders to that close family circle.

Despite the apparent scepticism towards language, this aesthetic position did not by any means exclude words or indeed visual elements from working alongside the music's meaning, but again use in the private circle was different from public deployment. What Mendelssohn was responding to in his famous remark about music's greater precision was a request for clarification concerning the 'right' descriptive titles to certain of his *Songs without Words*, and he hesitated to offer verbal correlates to the music as he found words unclear in this respect. But there is plenty of evidence that words and verbal meanings could be used in conjunction with music within the close circle, where they were less 'liable to be misunderstood'. This may even apply to the *Songs without Words*. A letter from Hensel to Mendelssohn of 7 September 1838 offers a tantalising glimpse of a sibling practice of 'texting' music, apparently a private amusement undertaken as children, whereby an existing instrumental piece or phrase would be fitted with a textual correlate.[21] It appears that such association between music and words may not have been uncommon in the Mendelssohn circle in the 1820s.

A prime example of such private musical communication, in Bartsch's view, is the cycle of six songs Hensel wrote in 1829 following the departure of her brother to England. The *Liederkreis, An Felix während seiner ersten Abwesenheit in England* (To Felix during his first absence in England), H-U236, takes rather further the idea of the earlier C minor Sonata (*Für Felix. In seiner Abwesenheit*) written five years earlier as Felix was recuperating at the Baltic Sea resort of Bad Doberan.[22] The poems, written for the purpose by their close friend Gustav Droysen, address the theme of departure, absence and longing for reunion, and a final joyous homecoming, in which the solitary voice of the first five songs is joined by two others in a family trio. Numerous internal references to Felix's music and current travels are given by the text, music, and even illustrations that Wilhelm Hensel provided on a fair copy of the score. Thus, one of the vignettes around the title shows a girl waiting (perhaps, like Fanny, composing) by a vine-clad wall, along with a tiny musical motive (Figure 2.1, top right of centre): the allusion is to Mendelssohn's earlier song 'Frage' (Question, 1827, subsequently published as Op. 9 No. 1), which had further served as the motto to his A minor String Quartet, Op. 13. The text (by 'H. Voss', a pseudonym of either Droysen or Mendelssohn himself) runs: 'Is it true, that you wait for me there, in the arbour, by the vine-clad wall? And ask the moonlight and the stars constantly about me too?' Fanny picks up on this textural association in her letter to Felix: 'The girl sits on a trellis, whose fruit will be known to you. Is it true that you once composed a lied and then composed a Quartet from this lied? And that others extract a great deal of substance from this Quartet and make constant allusions to it?'[23] And to complete the web of allusions employed across the different artistic media, Hensel's music reworks the dotted 'question' figure from Mendelssohn's song, already illustrated by Wilhelm, in her own second song.[24] Evocatively, the final statement is open-ended, the music trailing off, unfinished, on the dominant – a Romantic fragment, expressive of unfulfilled yearning, years before Robert Schumann would undertake a similar experiment in his song cycle *Dichterliebe*. The fifth song shifts the scene to the Scottish Highlands, which Felix was due to visit in August, and alludes verbally and musically to

Figure 2.1 Fanny Hensel, *Liederkreis*, 1829, first page, with vignettes by Wilhelm Hensel, including motive from Felix Mendelssohn's 'Frage', Op. 9 No. 1 (top centre-right). Bodleian Library, University of Oxford, GB-Ob, MS. M. D. Mendelssohn c. 22, fol. 22 r

his own atmospheric setting of Droysen's 'Wartend', also in B minor, composed just before leaving Berlin in April. The final 'Wiedersehen', whose trio of voices instantiate the theme of reunion, takes up a musical theme from her brother's recent

'Scottish' Sonata (the *Sonate écossaise* or Fantasy in F sharp minor, Op. 28), and is given visual illustration by Wilhelm by means of a boat sailing 'from the grey past into the golden future', alluding to Mendelssohn's *Calm Sea and Prosperous Voyage* Overture (1828), a work that held strong private significance for the circle in light of the journeying Felix.

The *Liederkreis* is small-scale, unassuming, and intimate: it makes no pretentions to greatness. Yet Felix, on receiving a copy in London, was quite overcome. As he relates in a letter to their younger brother Paul from 3 July 1829,

> Last night I played for myself the close of the 2nd [song] with the bird in the linden tree very quietly, and then did crazy things in my room, banged upon the table and may also have cried a lot. But then I played it on and on for quarter of an hour and now I know it very well. But as soon as I go to the piano and play it again, a shudder gets into me again, because I have never heard anything like it. It is the very innermost soul of music. And if I start to play the ending, I have to sing them all, for none is weaker. I can stop nowhere. At the end I sing the first once again, in which the words are spoken.[25]

An especially rich illustration of such interaction between musical, verbal, and pictorial elements is given over a decade later by Hensel's 1841 piano cycle, *Das Jahr*, written while she enjoyed an extended stay in Italy – a country she had long wished to visit – with her husband, the artist Wilhelm Hensel, and first published in 1989. A further, immaculately produced autograph copy discovered only in 2000 reveals poetic epigrams at the head of each of the twelve movements, linking the musical month of the year expressed in the music with an appropriate verbal stimulus taken from poets Goethe, Schiller, Uhland, Tieck, and Eichendorff. Furthermore, each month is written on different coloured paper, and her husband Wilhelm has provided pictorial vignettes around the opening bars of each. Yet all this was made for private eyes: there is no evidence that Hensel ever sought to reveal the extra-musical associations. Marian Wilson Kimber observes that:

> Fanny Hensel's provision of epigrams in *Das Jahr* is in keeping with the Mendelssohn family's aesthetic beliefs about the relationship of music and text ... Such epigrams would have been deemed too private to circulate outside her immediate sphere. During her first Italian journey, Hensel wrote to her

relatives in Berlin that she omitted any reference to the specific places that inspired her works when performing them, as 'that is only at home'.[26]

The close connection between music, words, and visual elements may indeed be a reason why Hensel would not seek to include the cycle, one of her most impressive achievements, when she came to select works for her first publications a few years later.

Receiving Beethoven

Much of the preceding account has focussed on the two elder siblings, Fanny and Felix. Although discussing a woman composer who has long been overshadowed by her brother with constant reference to the latter may seem questionable, is it unavoidable in the present case if we are to understand Hensel's life, music, and outlook: Felix Mendelssohn was very much the centre of Hensel's domestic musical circle. This is given direct visual expression in a celebrated drawing by Wilhelm Hensel, made in the summer of 1829 (Figure 2.2). 'Das Rad' – the wheel – depicts the lively circle of friends that had formed around the Mendelssohns and their comfortable home at Leipzigerstrasse 3, where the family had moved in 1825 and where Hensel would live until her death. Felix, at the time away in England, forms the centre (clad in a kilt and playing a pipe, in preparation for his impending visit to Scotland), from which sisters Fanny and Rebecka (depicted with fish-like tails, probably reflecting Felix's name for them – fish-otters), brother Paul, and their friends and romantic admirers radiate out. Wilhelm, seemingly caught on a string by Fanny, depicts himself on the periphery of the group; but might there not be a sense that it is actually he who is fishing, trying to draw the attractive mermaid out of Felix's orbit and into a new sphere? Just a few months later the two would wed, and Fanny's life would take a new path.[27]

There were, of course, others around them, and their younger siblings Rebecka and Paul, with whom they could share their musical enthusiasms: these included Eduard Rietz, Felix's violin teacher; Johann Gustav Droysen, their young classics tutor turned good friend and a future celebrated historian; Karl Klingemann, a trainee diplomat who was lodging with the Mendelssohns; Julius

Figure 2.2 Wilhelm Hensel, 'Das Rad' ('The Wheel'), 1829. Drawing, water-colour, pencil, gold, bronze. Mendelssohn-Archiv, Staatsbibliothek, Berlin

Schubring, a young theologian and lifelong friend; the music critic Adolph Bernhard Marx, a few years older but just starting out on his influential career; and several others whose orbit intersected for a longer or shorter period of time with the lively Mendelssohn household in the 1820s. And further afield, there were other figures who exerted a gravitational attraction on the Mendelssohn circle at this time too.

One of the most significant enthusiasms the Mendelssohn siblings shared was a passion for the music of Ludwig van Beethoven, and in particular the 'difficult' late works that were being composed in these very years and scarcely understood by contemporaries. This was a taste in which the Mendelssohn children departed from their elders: neither father Abraham nor teacher Zelter had much time for Beethoven, but for the younger generation this music was new, strange, deeply moving, and decidedly exciting to get to know. For her twentieth birthday in 1825, their friend Karl Klingemann presented Fanny with a copy of the newly published 'Hammerklavier' Sonata, Op. 106, along with a spoof letter purportedly from Beethoven himself in Vienna. In it, 'Beethoven' thanks Fanny for playing several of his works (evidently she was already tackling the Fourth and Fifth Piano Concertos and the 'Archduke' Trio at this time), and sends the mighty B flat major Sonata to her in the name of friendship, acknowledging that while most listeners will not like it, he can count on his 'true friends' alone to understand his 'most inward soul states'.[28] In case she is puzzled by the piece, its composer is sure their learned friend Marx will happily explain it.

Klingemann's teasing remark was well aimed. A. B. Marx would become one of the chief architects of the Beethoven cult and seems to have exerted a strong influence, particularly on the teenage Mendelssohn, in this period; sadly they later fell out, and Marx destroyed their correspondence, which would have given fascinating insight into the musical views of the circle at this formative time. But other surviving sources show something of the Beethoven enthusiasm of the family circle at the time. One of the most famous is a letter Mendelssohn wrote in February 1828 to a friend, the Swedish composer Adolf Lindblad. Ruefully Felix concedes that he, too, loves the Adagio of the 'Harp' Quartet (in E flat, Op. 74), which is 'so damned sentimental' it makes him inwardly cry. But he is especially drawn to the *Cavatina* from the Quartet in B flat, Op. 130 ('where the first violin sings, and the whole world sings with it'), and the C sharp minor Quartet, Op. 131, with its 'gloomy' opening fugue and magical shift to the remote key of D major in the following movement. 'You see, that is one of my points!' he exclaims – 'the relationship of all 4 or 3 or 2 or 1 movements of a sonata to each other and to their parts, so that from the simple beginning throughout the entire existence of such a piece one already knows the secret.'[29] Intriguingly, in two of her letters to her brother from the previous year, Hensel signs off not with her name but with three notes that form the incipit of Op. 131's fugal answer (C♯–E♯–F♯, an otherwise unusual choice of notes); as with many of the Mendelssohns' internal references, this is hard to make out, but may be as if she is taking the second violin part, answering a previous fugal entry of her brother.[30]

It seems that Fanny and Felix must have seen copies of some new Beethoven works from the publisher Schlesinger in Berlin even prior to first publication (Schlesinger also printed the *Berliner allgemeine musikalische Zeitung*, which Marx edited and turned into a mouthpiece for spreading the word of Beethoven); this, indeed, is the best explanation for the fact that Mendelssohn could allude to the elder composer's Op. 132 A minor Quartet in his own quartet in that key, Op. 13 (1827), the greater part of which must have been completed before Beethoven's work was issued by Schlesinger that autumn. In later decades, Beethoven would be the second most-performed composer (after her brother) in Hensel's semi-private *Sonntagsmusiken* (Sunday Musicales) at her home in Berlin.[31]

It is well known that several of Mendelssohn's compositions from this period were deeply influenced by Beethoven's music, especially his late works: foremost among these are the Piano Sonata Op. 6 (1826) and the String Quartets Op. 13 (1827) and 12 (1829), which all incorporate clear references or allusions to Beethoven's late sonatas and quartets. Hensel was equally drawn to this source. An early example of Beethovenian influence is seen in her *Sonata o Capriccio* in F minor for piano (H-U113, 1824), which as Larry Todd has shown takes its bearings from Beethoven's *Appassionata* Sonata (Op. 57) in the same key, while the *Sonata o Fantasia* in G minor for Cello and Piano (H-U238) probably owes something of its fantasia structure and unexpected return to its opening andante theme to Beethoven's own Cello Sonata Op. 102 No. 1.[32] But most of her larger-scale instrumental works from the following decade show a strong Beethovenian influence, foremost among them being the String Quartet. And in several cases, the sources of influence are mixed: both Hensel and Mendelssohn respond to each other's musical reactions to Beethoven, reading his music partly through their sibling's development of its compositional implications.[33]

The 'Easter' Sonata (1828)

A final case study that exemplifies many of the issues raised in this chapter and points forward to the String Quartet, the topic of the following five chapters, may be provided by a brief look at one of Hensel's most important works from this early period, the Sonata in A major, H-U235, christened by Hensel the 'Easter' Sonata. This piece has become a *cause célèbre* in the last decade since its rediscovery by Angela Mace, one that is revealing of the complexities of Hensel's reception. Moreover, it is an immensely accomplished work and has received little analytical scrutiny until now.

The intriguing background to the work's resurfacing can be briefly summarised.[34] A handful of references to an 'Easter-Sonata' (*Ostersonate*) by Hensel exist: a diary entry of hers from April 1829, a letter from Klingemann later that August relating that Felix played her sonata on board a ship in Liverpool, and her subsequent amused response to her brother a week later. The work was never published, however, and appeared to have been lost. Equally, there was no 'Easter' Sonata, or indeed missing sonata, known of by Felix. In 1972, a recording surfaced on a French record label of a *Sonate de Pâques* (Easter Sonata), purported to be by 'Mendelssohn' (Felix, not Fanny, was clearly implied in the male pronouns of the sleeve notes); the autograph score, however, remained in private hands.[35] Yet despite its evident 'Mendelssohnian' touches, no one else ever seems to have been convinced it really was by Felix Mendelssohn, and for nearly four decades the piece was almost entirely ignored. It is tellingly omitted from both the inventory John Michael Cooper compiled for Douglass Seaton's 2001 *Mendelssohn Companion* and Ralf Wehner's authoritative 2009 thematic catalogue of Mendelssohn's works.[36] Larry Todd's 2010 biography of Hensel put the pieces together and suggested the strong likelihood that the *Sonate de Pâques* recorded was in fact Fanny Hensel's *Easter Sonata*. And a year later, detective work on the part of Angela Mace, at that point a graduate student of Todd's, confirmed that this was indeed by Hensel. Having managed to track down the elusive manuscript in private hands, Mace confirmed that the handwriting was Hensel's, and the pagination was an exact match for the missing section of a bound volume of Hensel's works housed in the Berlin State Library's Mendelssohn Archives. The subsequent attention was exciting for Hensel research, but often not entirely accurate in its reporting in the media. This is not, it should be emphasised, a case of a piece long held to be a 'Mendelssohn masterpiece' being dramatically reattributed to his sister: no one had seriously believed the sonata was by Mendelssohn or for that matter a masterpiece; it had simply been ignored for decades. But it is revealing that until the 2010s a major work by Hensel was hiding in plain sight, and almost no one had any interest in it. That is until now, of course.

Quite apart from the sensational backstory, the *Easter Sonata* is also fascinating as a piece of music in its own right. A four-movement piano sonata dating from 1828, the work is not only one of the most substantial compositions she would ever come to write but also provides an insight into Hensel's compositional influences and her own, quite individual formal propensities at the age of twenty-two.

Even on first listening, the sonata's provenance in the Mendelssohn family circle of the later 1820s is unmistakable; it moves in the same orbit as her brother's piano sonatas from the preceding years, most pertinently the E major Sonata, Op. 6 (1826), but possesses a formal and thematic fluidity that is quite distinctively Henselian. Signs of Beethoven's later period run throughout: the Piano Sonatas in A major, Op. 101, E major, Op. 109, and especially A flat major, Op. 110 inform the first movement (with perhaps a nod to the slow movement of the 'Hammerklavier', Op. 106, too). This influence is amalgamated, however, with echoes of her brother's works from the preceding years, themselves no less indebted to Beethoven. Thus bars 6–8 strongly echo the continuation of the opening theme in Mendelssohn's Op. 6, the rippling left-hand quavers of Hensel's climbing secondary theme (bb. 34ff.) correspond to the transition in Felix's movement, and the shimmering diminished sevenths into which the end of the exposition dissolves match those at the close of his exposition. The second movement calls up another decisive influence on the siblings, Johann Sebastian Bach, with its austere E minor opening theme and subsequent B minor fugato;

the third movement, a characteristically 'Mendelssohnian' scherzo, prefigures the style of her brother's *Three Caprices*, Op. 16, written the following year, but is formally freer. The finale, a stormy sonata structure in A minor, eventually blows itself out, to be succeeded by the calm assurance of a Lutheran chorale, *Christe, Du Lamm Gottes*, whose phrases are interspersed with new material that strongly recalls the mood of the sonata's opening without in fact having been heard before. The procedure is redolent of what Mendelssohn does in his A minor Quartet (whose 'Frage' motive is all but cited in bb. 210–11, in the same key of A major) and the Fantasy on 'The Last Rose of Summer', Op. 14, which dates from the same period. Her brother's Op. 6 sonata – which ends by returning to the peaceful close of its opening movement – is further called up at this point.

Unlike her later string quartet, the outer movements relate more perceptibly to sonata form, but even here Hensel allows herself considerable freedom. The first movement, *Allegro assai moderato*, can for instance be divided without too much trouble into exposition, development, recapitulation, and coda sections, but in every case the boundaries are smoothed over. For a start, the movement begins with a gently rocking four-bar thematic idea in 9/8, before reverting to the 3/4 time signature in bar 5 in which the rest of the movement is written. But despite their thematic saliency, these opening bars are never heard again and consequently hold an ambiguous formal status within the movement. Although in tempo and ostensibly constituting a thematic initiating gesture, the first four bars are curiously in a different metre from the remaining movement and express an introductory function in the larger use made of them. Instead, the continuation phrase from bar 5 returns not just throughout the exposition but most importantly at bar 144 to initiate a recapitulation.[37] Despite the fact that it appears intrinsically to form a thematic continuation, and thus needs to be preceded by other material, this phrase effectively becomes the primary idea in the movement. The result is that the primary-theme material always appears to emerge from something that is already ongoing, creating a sense of continuity, a supple flowing back and forth across both small- and larger-scale formal divisions.

Just as the recapitulation leads seamlessly out of the development section, so the end of the exposition also blurs into the start of the development through a passage of diminished sevenths that dissolve any previously accumulated energy. The idea is plainly taken from the corresponding place in the first movement of Mendelssohn's Op. 6 sonata, yet in that work the diminished sevenths are obviously post-cadential, arising after a clear perfect cadence in the dominant key. In Hensel's sonata, the projected cadence at bar 88 is undermined through plagal motion and textural reduction, breaking the implied melodic line off on scale-degree 3; as a result, the exposition simply dissolves and runs into the following section without any real break. It is hard to pinpoint the moment in which the development starts: one can probably say around bar 100, but the process is continuous.

The final stages of the movement likewise run across sectional divisions. A coda might be heard to start from bar 191, with a cadential arrival in A major and the *fortissimo* return of the primary theme's continuation phrase, as if initiating a new thematic section (the passage effectively replaces the pre-cadential, though closing-theme-like, material from b. 69). But the cadential progression overshoots towards the subdominant via the introduction of a tonic seventh, and the entire phrase comes to serve as an expanded cadential progression securing the final, decisive cadence at bar 205. The diminished sevenths that follow, familiar from the end of the exposition, are here at last restored to their seemingly intrinsic post-cadential function.

One of the reasons why the movement seems hard to grasp formally is due to this continual blurring of sections and constant recycling of material. Even within sections, the unexpected recurrence of material from an earlier passage often disorientates anyone trying to follow the design with conventional formal schemes in mind. There is consequently the effect of a fantasy-like elaboration of ideas, each metamorphosing into others and recurring unexpectedly throughout. Yet for all the surface complication, the underlying formal framework of the sonata is actually quite firmly preserved by Hensel.

The A minor finale also reworks sonata elements to Hensel's own purposes. There is already ambiguity at the opening over where the exposition as such really begins, which may be in the first bar or alternatively in the ensuing thematic statement at bar 28, the preceding material thus serving as introduction. As the initial material returns both near the start of the ostensible development section (from bar 69) and in the recapitulation (from bar 120), it seems likely that it does belong to the main movement, though the second primary theme from bar 28 does seem tighter-knit and more coherent as a thematic entity. Furthermore, the transition following this theme's deceptive cadence into bar 49 is extremely brief: the perfect authentic cadence (PAC) into the dominant minor in bar 59 is followed by the return of the primary-theme material from bar 28, suggesting we have already reached the exposition's closing section. The implication is of a continuous exposition – that is, one without a clear secondary theme – whose second part following the initiation of transitional activity is minuscule in comparison with the first. Perhaps as a result of this basis in the primary theme and absence of clear contrasting material, the reprise has little functional role to play after the return of the transition passage at bar 163, and its material is gradually liquidated into a plain A minor sonority. Thus, the major-key coda that now emerges does not so much overcome as relieve the exhaustion of the preceding sonata movement. Melodic phrases of the familiar Easter chorale are interspersed with new material – recitative-like gestures – and phrases that strongly recall earlier movements while never quite becoming an exact quotation.[38] The sonata's plagal close may seem to derive from the hymn-like material heard, but it is also a recurring Hensel fingerprint.

Both middle movements, meanwhile, exhibit Hensel's remarkable and idiosyncratic manipulation of ternary form, a feature that will recur in the central movements of the quartet a few years later. The tripartite basis of the E minor Largo is on one level clear, with the opening material returning at bar 136 following the central fugal section starting at bar 47. But the tonal basis is still in a state of flux, and it is not until some while later, at bar 158, that the tonic E minor is resumed. Rather than a clear point of return, Hensel diffuses the reprise over an expanse of music by desynchronising thematic from harmonic structure, resulting in a sense of continual unfolding. This procedure is taken to an even more subtle level in the following Allegretto. Here, not only is the internal construction and syntax of the opening scherzo highly fluid, but the expected return of this section following the central trio (bb. 107–80) never quite materialises as it should. A reprise is signalled through the liquidation of the trio material over a long tonic pedal and reminders of the scherzo's head motive (b. 180), but this gives way to further retransitional rhetoric interspersed with more fragments of the opening phrase. As the music continues, more and more of the scherzo material is heard (the 6/4 at bar 224 momentarily seems to realign with the music from bar 24, for instance), but it always sounds provisional, expectant, or preparatory, and the reprise as such never really arrives. Instead of this, the music gradually fragments into tantalising dabs of E major harmony amidst the lengthening silence; the final tonic is not even cadentially secured but reached from a 6/4. Here the remarkable conception underlying the scherzo movement in Hensel's string quartet is fittingly foreshadowed.

Notes

1. Gesine Schröder, 'Fannys Studien', in Martina Helmig (ed.), *Fanny Hensel, geb. Mendelssohn Bartholdy: Das Werk* (Munich: edition text+kritik, 1997), pp. 27–32.
2. The exercises are published in R. Larry Todd, *Mendelssohn's Musical Education: A Study and Edition of His Exercises in Composition* (Cambridge: Cambridge University Press, 1983).
3. Hensel's 'Lied zum Geburtstag des Vaters', H-U2; Mendelssohn's 'Lied zum Geburtstage meines guten Vaters', K 1. A sonata in D major for two pianos possibly pre-dates Mendelssohn's song; see Peter Ward Jones, 'Mendelssohn's First Composition', in John Michael Cooper and Julie D. Prandi (eds.), *The Mendelssohns: Their Music in History* (Oxford: Oxford University Press, 2002), pp. 101–13.
4. Hans-Günter Klein, 'Similarities and Differences in the Artistic Development of Fanny and Felix Mendelssohn Bartholdy in a Family Context: Observations Based on the Early Berlin Autograph Volumes', in Cooper and Prandi (eds.), *The Mendelssohns*, pp. 233–43.
5. Sebastian Hensel, *Die Familie Mendelssohn 1729–1847: Nach Briefen und Tagebüchern*, 3 vols. (Berlin: B. Behr, 1879), vol. I, p. 97; English translation in *The Mendelssohn Family (1729–1847): From Letters and*

The 'Easter' Sonata (1828)

Journals, trans. Carl Klingemann [d.J.], 2 vols. (London: Sampson Low, 1882), vol. I, p. 82.

6. Ibid., vol. I, p. 117.

7. Angela R. Mace, 'Fanny Hensel, Felix Mendelssohn Bartholdy, and the Formation of the Mendelssohnian Style', PhD diss., Duke University, 2013, pp. 37, 38.

8. Annette Nubbemeyer, 'Die Klaviersonaten Fanny Hensels. Analytische Betrachtungen', in Beatrix Borchard and Monika Schwarz-Danuser (eds.), *Fanny Hensel geb. Mendelssohn Bartholdy: Komponieren zwischen Geselligskeitsideal und romantischer Musikästhetik* (Stuttgart: J. B. Metzler, 1999), pp. 90–119 at 95–6.

9. R. Larry Todd, 'On Stylistic Affinities in the Works of Fanny Hensel and Felix Mendelssohn Bartholdy', in Cooper and Prandi (eds.), *The Mendelssohns*, pp. 245–61 at 259.

10. Camilla Cai, 'Fanny Hensel's "Songs for Pianoforte" of 1836–37: Stylistic Interaction with Felix Mendelssohn', *Journal of Musical Research*, 14 (1994), 66–73.

11. Felix Mendelssohn Bartholdy to Fanny Hensel, Frankfurt, 24 June 1837. 'Ist es nicht seltsam, daß zuweilen musikalische Ideen in der Luft herum zu fliegen scheinen und sich da und dort niederlassen? ... Es ist gar zu lustig. Nebenbei ist es hübsch, daß unsre Gedanken einander so nahe bleiben.' Felix Mendelssohn Bartholdy, *Sämtliche Briefe*, ed. Helmut Loos, Wilhelm Seidel, et al., 12 vols. (Kassel: Bärenreiter, 2008–17), vol. V, p. 294.

12. See Mendelssohn's letter of 13–14 August 1829, *Sämtliche Briefe*, vol. I, p. 365; the matter is discussed further in Angela Mace Christian, '"Der Jüngling und Das Mädchen": Fanny Hensel, Felix Mendelssohn, and the *Zwölf Lieder*, Op. 9', in Aisling Kenny and Susan Wollenberg (eds.), *Women and the Nineteenth-Century Lied* (Farnham: Ashgate, 2015), pp. 63–84.

13. On the social inhibitions on Hensel's publishing, see especially Nancy B. Reich, 'The Power of Class: Fanny Hensel', in R. Larry Todd (ed.), *Mendelssohn and His World* (Princeton, NJ: Princeton University Press, 1991), pp. 86–99.

14. Niels Gade, letter of 14 October 1843, quoted in R. Larry Todd, *Fanny Hensel: The Other Mendelssohn* (New York: Oxford University Press, 2010), p. 300.

15. Unknown critic, *Allgemeine musikalische Zeitung*, 49 (1827), col. 382, quoted in Todd, *Fanny Hensel*, p. 349.

16. Mace, 'Fanny Hensel, Felix Mendelssohn Bartholdy', 38.

17. Mendelssohn, letter to Marc-André Souchay, 15 October 1842, *Sämtliche Briefe*, vol. IX, p. 74.

29

18. Thomas Christian Schmidt, *Die ästhetischen Grundlagen der Instrumentalmusik Felix Mendelssohn Bartholdys* (Stuttgart and Weimar: M & P, 1996), pp. 171–86.

19. Cornelia Bartsch in *Fanny Hensel, geb. Mendelssohn: Musik als Korrespondenz* (Kassel: Furore, 2007).

20. Cornelia Bartsch, 'Fanny Hensels einziges Streichquartett – ein Problemfall? Fanny Hensels Streichquartett zwischen Zuweisungen und Aneignung', in Claudia von Braunmühl (ed.), *Etablierte Wissenschaft und feministische Theorie im Dialog* (Berlin: Berliner Wissenschafts-Verlag, 2003), pp. 135–58, at p. 144; compare Schmidt, *Die ästhetischen Grundlagen der Instrumentalmusik Felix Mendelssohn Bartholdys*, p. 191.

21. Hensel to Mendelssohn, 7 September 1838, in Marcia Citron, *The Letters of Fanny Hensel to Felix Mendelssohn, Collected, Edited and Translated with Introductory Essays and Notes* (Stuyvesant, NY: Pendragon, 1987), p. 261 (English translation)/p. 547 (German original); see also Bartsch, *Musik als Korrespondenz*, pp. 331–2. This wider practice is described by Christopher Reynolds as one of 'texting' (see *Motives for Allusion: Context and Content in Nineteenth-Century Music* (Cambridge, MA: Harvard University Press, 2003), pp. 88–100); he gives further examples of this technique between the Mendelssohn siblings (pp. 94–5).

22. Bartsch, *Musik als Korrespondenz*, pp. 261–304. A much-compressed English version of this material is given in Cornelia Bartsch, 'Music as Correspondence', part of Beatrix Borchard and Cornelia Bartsch, 'Leipziger Straße Drei: Sites for Music', *Nineteenth-Century Music Review*, 4/2 (2007), 126–31.

23. Hensel, letter of 4–10 June 1829, in Citron, *The Letters of Fanny Hensel to Felix Mendelssohn*, p. 50/p. 403.

24. As Bartsch observes, 'the main motif of her song, which has the same number of bars as his, appears exactly the same number of times as the thematic motto of his song' ('Music as Correspondence', p. 128). This is not the only time the siblings would respond to the musical 'question' motive (which indeed has a long prehistory even prior to the related 'Muss es sein' motive in the finale of Beethoven's Quartet Op. 135); Mendelssohn's own 'Geständniss', placed next to 'Frage' as Op. 9 No. 2, also reworks this motive, to which Hensel would respond in turn in 'Genesungsfeier', H-U252, written to celebrate their sister Rebecka's convalescence from measles in 1830.

25. Mendelssohn, letter to Paul Mendelssohn Bartholdy, 3 July 1829, *Sämtliche Briefe*, vol. I, p. 326.

26. Marian Wilson Kimber, 'Fanny Hensel's Seasons of Life: Poetic Epigrams, Vignettes, and Meaning in *Das Jahr*', *Journal of Musicological Research*, 27 (2008), 359–95, at pp. 369, 370–1.

27. On Hensel's struggle to wrest herself from her close ties to her brother at this time, see Angela Mace Christian, 'Sibling Love and the Daemonic: Contradictions in the Relationship between Felix and Fanny Mendelssohn', in Benedict Taylor (ed.), *Rethinking Mendelssohn* (New York: Oxford University Press, 2020), pp. 140–57.

28. See Todd, *Fanny Hensel*, p. 89. Eric Werner, who reproduces the letter in his *Mendelssohn: A New Image of the Composer and His Age*, trans. Dika Newlin (London: Free Press of Glencoe, 1963), pp. 108–9, mistakenly attributes the authorship to Felix.

29. Mendelssohn, letter to Adolf Lindblad, 19(?) February 1828, in *Sämtliche Briefe*, vol. 1, pp. 240–1.

30. Letters from Hensel to Mendelssohn, 16 February 1827 and undated, in Citron, *The Letters of Fanny Hensel*, pp. 19–20/382–3; the clef is not written by Hensel, but given the pitches treble seems most plausible. It is interesting that Hensel does not continue onto the fourth note, a D♮ that foreshadows the key of the second movement – a 'secret' connection behind the shift that her brother seems to relish.

31. See Angela R. Mace, 'Fanny Hensel, Felix Mendelssohn Bartholdy', p. 192; also Christian Lambour, 'Fanny Hensel als Beethoven-Interpretin', in Betina Brand and Martina Helmig (eds.), *Maßstab Beethoven? Komponistinnen im Schatten des Geniekults* (Munich: edition text+kritik, 2001), pp. 106–19.

32. Todd, *Fanny Hensel*, pp. 80, 137.

33. Thus, Hensel's Fugue in E flat (H-U273, 1834), which responds to the fugue in the finale of Beethoven's Piano Sonata in A flat, Op. 110, is in turn responded to by Mendelssohn in his Fugue in A flat, Op. 35 No. 4 (1835). See Todd, *Fanny Hensel*, p. 178.

34. The account here draws on Mace, 'Fanny Hensel, Felix Mendelssohn Bartholdy', pp. 42–53, and Todd, *Fanny Hensel*, pp. 135–7; a fuller account is published in Angela Mace Christian, 'The *Easter Sonata* of Fanny Mendelssohn (1828)', *Journal of Musicological Research*, 41/3 (2022), 182–209.

35. Cassiopée Records 369182, performed by the pianist Eric Heidsieck.

36. John Michael Cooper, 'Mendelssohn's Works: Prolegomenon to a Comprehensive Inventory', in Douglass Seaton (ed.), *The Mendelssohn Companion* (Westport, CT: Greenwood Press, 2001); Ralf Wehner, *Felix Mendelssohn Bartholdy: Thematisch-systematisches Verzeichnis der musikalischen Werke* (Wiesbaden: Breitkopf und Härtel, 2009). Conversely, however, Hensel scholars were not drawn to the work recorded either; Hellwig-Unruh's 2000

thematic catalogue of Hensel's works simply gives the piece as 'lost' (Renate Hellwig-Unruh, *Fanny Hensel geb. Mendelssohn Bartholdy: Thematisches Verzeichnis der Kompositionen* (Adliswil: Edition Kunzelmann, 2000), p. 211).

37. Although the start seems to correspond to b. 5, the recapitulation in fact resumes the expositional cycle from the equivalent of b. 23, thus enabling considerable truncation of the exposition.

38. These intermovement allusions are strongest in the phrase from b. 207 to b. 214, which manages to evoke the three preceding movements in turn while still recalling works of Hensel's brother (the Sonata Op. 6 and the 'Frage' motive from Op. 9 No. 1/Op. 13, also previously referenced in Hensel's second movement), all without ever constituting literal references.

3

GENESIS AND PRIVATE RECEPTION

The Unfinished Piano Sonata in E flat (1829)

On 10 April 1829, the day her brother Felix departed on his travels, Fanny embarked upon her *Liederkreis, To Felix during His First Absence in England*. The words for this highly personal creation were penned by Gustav Droysen, with whom Fanny was getting on very well in this period of Felix's absence; too well perhaps for Wilhelm Hensel's liking, since it seems there was a mild contretemps between the betrothed couple later that summer. (Wilhelm, who had first met Fanny as far back as 1821, had been kept at arm's-length by her parents for quite some time, including a forced separation of five years designed to test his resolve and true feelings for her; it is perhaps understandable that he might have felt oversensitive about any perceived threat to their union this close to their planned wedding.) Following the song cycle, Fanny and Droysen had discussed collaborating on a more substantial cycle on the topic of the Lorelei and had then planned an elaborate *scena* for her parents' silver wedding anniversary at the end of the year. This was evidently too much for her husband-to-be. To placate Wilhelm, Fanny wrote to him that September, assuring him that she would return the text for the new *scena* back to Droysen and have no more to do with the project. Moreover, she reassures him, 'I will compose no more for voice, at least nothing from new poets personally known to me, least of all from Droysen. I'll stick with instrumental music; I can confide to it what I will; it is discreet.'[1] They were finally married a few weeks later, on 3 October 1829. Felix, who had dearly wanted to be there for the wedding, was unable to return: a bad leg injury detained him in England for over two months more, and he would arrive in Berlin only on 7 December.

In this period, the newly married Fanny Hensel's attention turned to another piano sonata – more appropriate, more discreet, perhaps, for the state of matrimony. Three movements exist in manuscript from this autumn: an *Adagio* in E flat, an Intermezzo marked *Allegretto* in C minor, and a *Largo molto* in A flat.[2] It is generally assumed that these movements belong to an unfinished sonata in E flat major, following Hensel's stated intention in a letter to her brother from the end of September that the first work after her marriage would be a sonata, although the word 'Sonate' is not in fact written on the manuscript.[3] There is also no finale: the work appears to have been left incomplete. The second and third movements are dated 9 and 12 November 1829 respectively; an earlier four-bar sketch of the former, marked 'Scherzo', has also survived, dated 9 May 1829. The date for the first movement has been partially cut off in binding. Renate Hellwig-Unruh has argued that the number 18 still visible most likely indicates 18 October, given the dates of the two movements that follow in the manuscript. 18 September would be too early, given that Hensel speaks of the sonata ten days later as a future project; moreover the close ties of Hensel's *Adagio* to the opening movement of Mendelssohn's own E flat Quartet, completed in London on 14 September and sent to his family later that month, strongly imply Hensel had started writing her movement only after receiving this copy.[4]

The incomplete Piano Sonata, catalogued as H-U246, is the source for two of the four movements of the String Quartet written five years later in 1834. The sonata's opening *Adagio* was taken over with only minor modifications to serve as the opening movement of the quartet. Curiously, both movements are the same length, seventy-seven bars, though this resemblance disguises deleted and newly added bars made in the process.[5] The second movement intermezzo was also incorporated into the new work, but here Hensel expanded her original fifty-three bars through the addition of a new trio section, which is followed by a modified return of the opening, resulting in a much more substantial 173-bar movement. In the process, the title 'intermezzo' was also dropped, Hensel keeping simply the *Allegretto* tempo designation. The A flat major *Largo molto*, on the other hand, was discarded, replaced in the quartet by a new 'Romanza', nominally in G minor, and a new finale in E flat composed.

The String Quartet: Motivations and Sources

Why did Hensel come to write a string quartet in 1834? There was a large domestic market for accessible pieces for string quartet in this period – arrangements of popular operatic airs, well-crafted and attractive quartets from the likes of Louis Spohr and George Onslow that were grateful for accomplished amateur performers to play – but Hensel was not a string player herself, and there is no suggestion that the piece was written for her own performance or that of anyone else in her immediate surroundings.[6] She was not publishing at this time and would hardly have been looking to popular sales for generating income. Her quartet clearly takes its place in another tradition, that which saw the string quartet as a pinnacle of musical thinking and an exacting demonstration of compositional craft – the quartet for connoisseurs. 'The most refined, as well as the most difficult of all kinds of composition', Carl Czerny asserted around this time, 'the quartet remains the most hazardous, but at the same time also, the most honourable touchstone for a composer.'[7] Such a tradition was closely associated with the Viennese heritage of Haydn, Mozart, and especially Beethoven; it was also very much linked, as we saw earlier, to a 'masculine' sphere, despite the private nature of the chamber-music medium.

It is conspicuous that the string quartet does not feature in the chamber works of the 1820s in which Hensel had tried out her craft, though the piano quartet – a much less loaded genre – does. Even her brother Felix had been wary of approaching the string quartet too soon; several chamber works for piano and strings (including a piano trio and two piano quartets) had been completed before he would embark upon his first string quartet (in E flat, MWV R18, 1823), and his first published examples (Op. 12 and 13, written in 1829 and 1827) post-date numerous chamber works composed for different forces (the Piano Quartets Opp. 1–3, a String Octet, Op. 20, and Quintet, Op. 18). Hensel, then, was embarking upon an ambitious project, one in which she probably would have known no precedent for a woman composer to do so. She had nevertheless been working her way in this direction: two years earlier, in 1832, Hensel had written her first purely orchestral work, the Overture in C, expanding her compositional range into another genre normally reserved for men (and also very successfully taken over by her brother), which followed on the heels of three orchestral cantatas (*Lobgesang*, *Hiob*, and the *Choleramusik*, all 1831) and a dramatic scene for soprano and orchestra, *Hero und Leander* (1831–2).

Renate Hellwig-Unruh thinks it is likely that the immediate stimulus for writing a quartet might have actually come from Felix Mendelssohn. In May 1834, Hensel, at a bit of a loose end following a private run through of her overture and looking for a new challenge, asked her brother to propose a new compositional task: 'Give me something to compose, but not the history of the world, or the Thirty-Years War, or the time of the popes, or the island of Australia, but something really useful and solid.'[8] There is no written record of his response, but later that summer, at the end of August, Mendelssohn visited his sister at the family home in Berlin and stayed for a month, more or less coinciding with the time she began work on the quartet (the outer movements are dated 26 August and 23 October 1834 respectively; Mendelssohn arrived on 29 August and stayed until 30 September).[9] Whether or not the idea came from him, at the very least, his presence alongside her for a month during the creation of the quartet points to him being party to her new enterprise, and subsequent letters reveal he already knew parts of the quartet before she sent him a copy of the finished piece later that winter.

The quartet has come down to us only in Hensel's autograph score; it was never published in her lifetime, and neither a copy she sent to her brother that Christmas nor parts which presumably had been prepared for a private run-through in November have survived. Besides the manuscript for the earlier E flat Piano Sonata, in which the first two movements originated, there are a couple of undated sketches on two staves for the material that would be used for the new trio, and another undated sketch, on a single stave, for the main theme of the finale. Hellwig-Unruh surmises from the handwriting and ink that these are likely to have been written a while after the sonata, probably in the summer of 1834 as Hensel started thinking about the work again, though this cannot be known for certain.[10] The autograph, housed in the Berlin Staatsbibliothek, is for the most part quite neatly written, but there are numerous corrections added, bars crossed out, replacement pages, and several passages in which new variants have been pasted over (see Figure 5.1 below for an illustration).[11] We know from a letter of 4 November that Hensel incorporated changes to the second movement (which she refers to as the 'scherzo') following her brother's advice, but presumably this had been given in person in September while the two were together, and the revisions go beyond this movement.[12]

Unsurprisingly, the two sections taken over from the Piano Sonata – the Adagio and opening of the Allegretto – show minimal corrections, these being reserved for a couple of places where Hensel changes her mind about which octave to place a line or how the voices should be divided between the instruments. Alongside the pedal markings visible in the earlier manuscript, these lend weight to the supposition that the piano sonata was not in fact conceived as a short-score for an eventual quartet (an otherwise attractive idea, given that the primary models for this movement are string quartets). The main revisions are found in the newly written parts – the trio of the second movement, the third-movement Romanza – while an extra page has been inserted in the finale. The second and third movements begin on the same page as the end of the preceding movement, leaving no doubt as to the order intended and that they belong to the same work. The work is entitled (in German) 'Quartet for 2 Violins, Viola and Cello, composed by F. Hensel', though the French term 'Quatuor' is written above the first page of the score. Two editions have been published of the quartet: in 1988 from Breitkopf und Härtel, and one year later from Furore Verlag, reissued in a revised edition in 1997.[13] The two show some discrepancies in editorial interpretation and intervention, most critically in the second movement (discussed in Chapter 5).

Fraternal Reception: The Critical Exchange of 1835

Soon after finishing the quartet on 23 October, Hensel wrote to her brother informing him of its completion and saying that she was going to try it out that week.[14] Following this, Hensel planned to send a copy to him for Christmas but did not post it in time (the letter was started on 30 November but completed only on Christmas Day). It took Mendelssohn another month to get back with his reaction to the finished piece. Mendelssohn's letter of 30 January 1835 is effectively the only response to Hensel's quartet for a century and a half. We do not know of any other reception from this time; given that the quartet seems to have been played only in private and circulated solely between the two siblings, it is unlikely anyone outside Hensel's immediate family and those performers involved in the private run-through would have seen or heard it. This trial run at Hensel's Berlin home may have been the only time it was performed for nearly 150 years. It is also possible Mendelssohn had the quartet played privately, as his sister requested, but there is no record of this.

It is a remarkable letter: despite the opening understatement ('a small critical remark'), it constitutes the most extensive statement on matters of musical form from a composer who was extremely reticent to theorise and distrusted music criticism. Despite Mendelssohn's evident regard for his sister's music, his criticism may also seem surprisingly pointed. It will be quoted at length here.

Dear Fenchel [Mendelssohn's pet name for his sister; literally 'fennel'],
I've already wanted for four days to write and thank you for the quartet, and never got round to it; only today have I managed. I have just played it through again to myself and thank you from my heart for it. My favourite movement is the C minor Scherzo as before, but the theme of the Romanza also pleases me very much. If you will permit me a small critical remark, it would concern the compositional style [*Schreibart*] of the whole or, if you like, the form [*Form*]. I would like that you pay more heed to a certain form, namely in the modulations – it is perfectly all right to shatter such a form, but it is the contents themselves which must shatter it, through inner necessity [*innere Nothwendigkeit*]; without this, such new or unusual formal turns and modulations only make the piece more vague and diffuse. I have noticed the same mistake in several of my recent things, and therefore can speak of it well, though I don't know whether I can do better. In the first movement – which despite this is so dear to me – I had already noticed this in Berlin, I believe, but it is apparent to me in the others too. To give an example, I would like to cite merely the themes and cadences, which are, until the last movement, in no key at all [*in gar keiner Tonart*], and even if that might, for

instance, appear necessary in the first movement, nevertheless it is too much and becomes a mannerism when it also arises in the others. And with the first movement it is not the swaying between E flat major and C minor that creates this, for that is very nice; but the cadence that follows is in F minor, and the start of the quavers in F minor, and then the fermata in F minor, and the viola (good as it is) in F major – this is what I mean. Similarly, the end of the scherzo, which is actually not in a key, and the middle, and likewise the start of the following Romanza, and its middle, that modulates first here and then there. – Don't take this badly, little sister [*Gerelein* – another pet name], and don't take me for a Philistine – I'm not, and believe I'm right when I have more respect than before for form, and proper [*ordentlicher*] working, and whatever else the technical terms may be called. Send me something nice soon, or else I'll think that you want to strike me dead as a reviewer.[15]

The two siblings were each other's closest critics, and neither would shy away from expressing their true thoughts on the other's works. Still, Hensel may have been slightly taken aback at the scale of the criticism. It was not until 17 February 1835, following another letter from her brother, that she would respond.

She starts by thanking him for his recent letters and addresses first the choral cantatas Mendelssohn mentions later on in his letter. Praising much of the music, she nevertheless gives her brother a taste of his own medicine. The last movement of his *Ach Gott vom Himmel sieh' darein* is just as tonally wayward as he had charged her music as being, moving from F sharp minor via A minor to C major, as remote a progression as possible, and yet here Hensel believes the text demanded 'an extremely constant and steadfast musical setting'. In Mendelssohn's sacred cantatas, moreover, she finds 'something simplistic, which doesn't appear entirely natural … childlike, but also something childish'. She assures him this is in no way a critical tit-for-tat.[16] Hensel then turns to the matter of the quartet:

Thanks for the proper [*ordentliche*] critique of my quartet. Will you have it played once? You know, I find we now write each other very proper [*ordentliche*] letters, perhaps not quite so jolly as those I wrote sitting together with Beckchen (Rebecka), taking the quill out of each other's hand, but rationally over proper [*ordentliche*] objects.[17] It is fine by me if it stays like this.

One suspects the ironic repetition of her brother's adjective *ordentliche* (proper, orderly) is in part a defensive reaction: note the contrast offered by the more fun-loving family environment Hensel enjoyed with her sister Rebecka, an implicit reproach to her brother's grown-up, *ordentliche* meanness.[18] The suggestion slipped in that he actually hears the piece played not only offers a counter-criticism but also perhaps points to an enduring belief that the quartet possesses at least some value. After a few comments on her musical activities during the last weeks, Hensel resumes discussion of compositional matters a few lines later, now offering some concession to the critique of her work, albeit choosing to frame this in slightly different terms than those offered by her brother:

I have made an aria for soprano that would please you better with regard to form and modulation, which it observes fairly strictly, and I had even finished it before you wrote to me. I was thinking over how I, actually not at all an eccentric or hypersentimental person, could have come to this soft compositional style [*weichlichen Schreibart*]? I think it comes from the fact that both of us were young exactly during Beethoven's last years, and his manner and way was thus easily taken up in us. Yet it is simply too moving and touching [*rührend und eindringlich*]. You have lived through it and worked your way through it, and I have remained stuck within it, but without the strength through which alone the tenderness can and should be supported. This is also why I believe that you haven't quite put your finger or expressed the right point on me. It is not so much the compositional style [*Schreibart*] that is lacking as a particular principle of life [*Lebensprinzip*], and as a consequence of this lack my longer things die in their youth of decrepitude; I am missing the strength to sustain ideas properly, to give them the necessary consistency. Therefore songs suit me best, in which in any case an attractive idea without much strength for development suffices.[19]

Several points could be taken from the preceding exchange:

- First of all, it is worth considering whether sister and brother might in reality be quite distinct from each other in their compositional outlook. The criticisms of each other's works are perfectly cogent on their own terms, but arguably are the result of divergent standpoints more than anything else. As Annegret Huber has argued, this tension between different aesthetic stances also simmers below the surface in many of their exchanges over the following decade: Mendelssohn chides his sister for harmonic waywardness and lack of discipline, Hensel reproaches her brother for excessive simplicity.[20] Despite the talk of a common Mendelssohnian style, there are real musical differences between Fanny Hensel and Felix Mendelssohn.

- Mendelssohn's criticism arguably says as much about his own aesthetic concerns at the time as about the worth of his sister's quartet. This was a period in which he was realigning his aesthetic priorities, moving away from the more experimental and formally radical works of his teenage years, a time when Beethoven's late style had been a decisive influence, and towards a more disciplined and self-consciously retrained mode of composition ('proper', *ordentlich*). Hensel points to just this in commenting on how he has lived and worked through Beethoven's last period, while she is still in the midst of this. Mendelssohn was also increasingly distrustful of the younger generation of composers and what he considered their constant striving for novelty and sentimental effusiveness (Rainer Cadenbach speaks in this context of an almost 'allergic reaction' on Mendelssohn's part to the Romantic tendencies he had encountered in Paris in 1832).[21] It also follows that the formal liberties and far-flung tonal excursions he might have permitted in the 1820s were now becoming suspect: music that Mendelssohn might have responded to positively in 1829 he would have greater reservations about by 1835. As much as criticising his sister, Mendelssohn may well be working through his own evolving compositional ideals.
- It should also be mentioned that this is not a one-off or even the first instance of crossed critical views between the two. The previous year, in April 1834, Mendelssohn had been mildly exasperated when his sister had not 'understood' his overture to *The Tale of the Fair Melusina*, asking him what story he had in mind. He would have expected his big sister, his 'ideal listener', to have understood the music without needing to ask for verbal clarification.[22] Moreover, later that summer Hensel had responded negatively to revisions he had made to the 'Italian' Symphony, telling him bluntly that she preferred the original version and she didn't understand why he had to change what was so nice the first time (audiences have generally agreed with her). The criticism of her quartet offered by Mendelssohn is thus not an unprovoked blow; neither is it quite as brutal as might appear out of context. But more importantly, it shows that even these two musical soulmates were not quite as unanimous in their views as they might first have seemed. They were growing further apart in aesthetic ideals in this period, and we see clear signs of this in Mendelssohn's criticism. Just as Hensel wasn't able to follow her brother's story in his overture, so, perhaps, was Mendelssohn unable to follow his sister's logic in the quartet.
- Some of the specific terms and concepts used by the two are not self-explanatory and need careful consideration before being employed in present-day discussion. When Mendelssohn uses the word 'form', for instance, he does not mean anything like what we might think of as

form in the sense of schematic type or 'mould' (ternary form, sonata form, etc.). Rather, it points to how tonal and especially cadential structure is decisive for Mendelssohn's conception of what constitutes form. When the cadences at the end of thematic statements conflict too often with the ostensible underlying key of the movement, then the sense of larger tonal structure can be compromised – hence his claim that much of Hensel's quartet is 'in no key at all' (by which he is clearly not suggesting it is 'atonal' in the twentieth-century sense). 'Innere Nothwendigkeit' is another tricky term, one of those typical, seemingly loose phrases often employed by writers in that age that might seem to appeal to vague notions of spiritual unity and organicism.[23] As I will suggest in the following chapter, it might be more helpful to think of the idea in terms of a perceived 'inevitability' of musical events rather than 'inner necessity', pointing to a greater emphasis in Mendelssohn's aesthetics on establishing a dialogue with generic expectations.[24]

• What Hensel means when she writes *Lebensprinzip* (principle of life, living principle) is perhaps most puzzling of all. As Cadenbach has suggested, there are several different possible meanings of the term, and any translation will furthermore affect how this is understood.[25] Does Hensel mean that her personal situation – as a woman – had limited her access to those musical activities that her brother has enjoyed, restricting her to a private sphere of music-making that inevitably compromised her compositional output? Or more specifically, might it admit a want of regular practice and consequently lack of experience in composing in larger genres? Could this even relate to the music's own 'living principle', as the following discussion of her music 'dying in its youth' – an organicist metaphor for not being able to sustain an idea – shows? It is hardly clear. What we might take away from this brief discussion is how our relation to a former age's technical vocabulary and horizon of expectations is not always as straightforward as it might seem.

These points are worth bearing in mind throughout the discussion of Hensel's quartet in the following four chapters. We do not of course have to see the work through her brother's eyes or concur with the evaluation he gives, though his comments do highlight some notable features of the quartet. Equally, we need not entirely agree with Hensel, lacking self-confidence when venturing out into instrumental music and easily discouraged by her esteemed musical sibling, on the matter of what she perceives as her weakness. Two views hardly make up a substantial reception history. Fortunately, this offers a present-day audience ample scope for considering the work afresh.

Notes

1. Fanny Mendelssohn, letter to Wilhelm Hensel, probably middle of September 1829, in Martina Helmig and Annette Maurer (eds.), 'Fanny Mendelssohn Bartholdy und Wilhelm Hensel: Briefe aus der Verlobungszeit', in Martina Helmig (ed.), *Fanny Hensel, geb. Mendelssohn Bartholdy: Das Werk* (Munich: edition text+kritik, 1997), p. 155.

2. The manuscript is housed in the Staatsbibliothek Berlin, DB-SB, MA Depos. Lohs 4, 73–6.

3. See letter from Fanny Mendelssohn to Felix Mendelssohn, (28 and) 29 September 1829, in Marcia Citron, *The Letters of Fanny Hensel to Felix Mendelssohn, Collected, Edited and Translated with Introductory Essays and Notes* (Stuyvesant, NY: Pendragon, 1987), p. 88 (English translation)/p. 428 (German original).

4. Renate Hellwig-Unruh, 'Zur Entstehung von Fanny Hensels Streichquartett in Es-Dur (1829/34)', in Beatrix Borchard and Monika Schwarz-Danuser (eds.), *Fanny Hensel geb. Mendelssohn Bartholdy: Komponieren zwischen Geselligskeitsideal und romantischer Musikästhetik* (Stuttgart: J. B. Metzler, 1999), pp. 124–8.

5. See Angela R. Mace, 'Fanny Hensel, Felix Mendelssohn Bartholdy, and the Formation of the Mendelssohnian Style', PhD diss., Duke University, 2013, pp. 196–7.

6. See Marie Sumner Lott, *The Social Worlds of Nineteenth-Century Chamber Music* (Urbana: University of Illinois Press, 2015).

7. Carl Czerny, *School of Practical Composition: Complete Treatise on the Composition of All Kinds of Music*, Opus 600, trans. John Bishop, 3 vols. (London: R. Cocks & Co., 1848), vol. II, p. 6. The treatise was probably written around 1840.

8. Letter from Fanny Hensel to Felix Mendelssohn, 11 May 1834, Citron, *The Letters of Fanny Hensel*, p. 140/p. 465.

9. Hellwig-Unruh, 'Zur Entstehung von Fanny Hensels Streichquartett', p. 123; Hensel in *Fanny Hensel: Tagebücher*, ed. Hans-Günter Klein and Rudolf Elvers (Wiesbaden: Breitkopf & Härtel, 2002), pp. 59–61.

10. Hellwig-Unruh, 'Zur Entstehung von Fanny Hensels Streichquartett', p. 127; a helpful discussion of the sources is given on pp. 124–34, on which the present account partly draws.

11. MA Ms 43; a scan is freely available online: https://digital.staatsbibliothek-berlin.de/werkansicht/?PPN=PPN1724626299.

12. Letter 4 November 1834, Citron, *The Letters of Fanny Hensel*, p. 154/p. 475.

13. Fanny Hensel, *Streichquartett Es-dur (Kammermusik-Bibliothek 2255)*, ed. Günter Marx (Wiesbaden: Breitkopf und Härtel, 1988) and Fanny Hensel-Mendelssohn, *Streichquartett Es-Dur (fue 121)*,

ed. Renate Eggebrecht-Kupsa (Kassel: Furore, 1989, 2nd rev. ed. 1997).

14. Letter 4 November 1834, Citron, *The Letters of Fanny Hensel*, p. 154/p. 475.

15. Felix Mendelssohn, letter to Fanny Hensel, 30 January 1835, in *Sämtliche Briefe*, ed. Helmut Loos, Wilhelm Seidel, et al., 12 vols. (Kassel: Bärenreiter, 2008–17), vol. IV, pp. 155–6.

16. Fanny Hensel, letter of 17 February 1835, in Citron, *The Letters of Fanny Hensel*, pp. 489–90 (an alternative English translation is given on pp. 173–4).

17. Earlier letters (e.g. one postmarked 25 October 1828, ibid., pp. 21–2/ pp. 383–5) show Fanny and Rebecka taking turns to write sentences to their brother.

18. Nevertheless, Hensel also employs the term *ordentliche* in other correspondence from this time, suggesting she was aware (and possibly enjoyed the fact) that her letters could appear disorderly in topics and treatment.

19. Hensel, letter of 17 February 1835, in Citron, *The Letters of Fanny Hensel*, pp. 489–90 (an alternative English translation to mine is given on pp. 173–4).

20. Annegret Huber, 'Das Konzept der Montage als analytische Kategorie. Fanny Hensels Metaphernspiel um "Jugend/Altersschwäche" in neuem Licht', in *Digitale Festschrift für Beatrix Borchard zum 65. Geburtstag* (2016), formerly at https://mugi.hfmt-hamburg.de/ BeatrixBorchard/index.html%3Fp=59.html.

21. Rainer Cadenbach, '"Die weichliche Schreibart", "Beethovens letzte Jahre" und "ein gewisses Lebensprinzip": Perspektiven auf Fanny Hensels spätes Streichquartett (1834)', in Borchard and Schwarz-Danuser (eds.), *Fanny Hensel*, pp. 141–64 at 142.

22. See Benedict Taylor, *Mendelssohn, Time and Memory: The Romantic Conception of Cyclic Form* (Cambridge: Cambridge University Press, 2011), pp. 220–6.

23. Ironically, a lack of 'inner necessity' was a charge later levelled at Mendelssohn's *Lobgesang*: see John Michael Cooper, '"Inner Necessity": Fabulation, Frame, and Musical Memory in Mendelssohn's *Lobgesang*', in Benedict Taylor (ed.), *Rethinking Mendelssohn* (New York: Oxford University Press, 2020), pp. 60–90 at 61.

24. I am grateful to Thomas Schmidt for suggesting this interpretation.

25. Cadenbach, 'Die weichliche Schreibart', pp. 149–52.

4

FIRST MOVEMENT

Adagio ma non troppo

Hensel's individuality is readily demonstrated by the opening movement to her quartet. This *Adagio ma non troppo* initially bears the hallmarks of a slow introduction: indeed, the slow introductions to earlier quartets in the same key by Beethoven (the 'Harp', Op. 74, marked *Poco Adagio*) and Mendelssohn (Op. 12, similarly designated *Adagio non troppo*) are called to mind. Beyond the identical key and time signatures and the comparable tempo designations, the three quartets even share the same opening rhythmic motive (minim, dotted crotchet, quaver). Unlike those works, however, Hensel's Adagio constitutes a movement in its own right: there is no main movement that follows. Rather than a small-scale introduction to something else, these seventy-seven bars form the first of the quartet's four movements. Furthermore, the design of her Adagio bears little resemblance to customary schematic types, most pertinently first-movement sonata form. The absence of a sonata-form opening movement is highly unusual at this time for the quartet genre, as most commentators have noted. But there is one obvious precedent for Hensel, namely Beethoven's String Quartet in C sharp minor Op. 131 of 1826, a piece that held particular fascination for Hensel and her brother in the late 1820s. In Beethoven's work, a fugal *Adagio ma non troppo e molto espressivo* forms the opening part of a cycle of seven movements of diverse lengths, only the last of which is a sonata-based structure. Hensel's quartet adopts a more familiar four-movement layout, with a scherzo-like second movement, slow third movement, and *Allegro molto vivace* rondo finale. The resulting design in fact suggests something of the four-movement slow–fast–slow–fast layout of the

45

early eighteenth-century Italian sonata, reinterpreted through a quite modern sensibility (several commentators have pointed to the influence of the Romantic character piece in the diverse styles of the different movements). Just as Beethoven had experimented in his late works with different numbers of movements and suggestions of earlier generic traditions – his String Quartet in B flat major, Op. 130, calls up the model of the eighteenth-century divertimento, for instance – so Hensel offers her own novel reinterpretation of the possibilities of the string quartet as a genre, linking it both back to baroque precursors and forward to the contemporary practice of the 1830s.

Formally, the opening movement appears quite free, being generated more through the elaboration of the thematic ideas presented than by any dialogue with a generic design. Tonally the movement is also highly elusive. Although E flat major is implied from the beginning, no cadence is given in this key until the final bar. Instead of this, related keys – especially those in the contrasting mode, C minor and F minor – are emphasised, before the attainment of its dominant in the final third will eventually lead to the confirmation of the tonic E flat at the end. It is this non-generic formal design and tonally exploratory quality that imbues the Adagio with the typical rhetoric of an introduction, just as it is responsible for its frequent characterisation as fantasia-like. In fact, the formal and expressive idea of the movement can best be understood as a search for a stable tonic, state of rest, or homecoming – one that is repeatedly denied, before being granted at the very end.

The Opening Paradigm

The Adagio is oriented around the thematic idea presented at the outset (Example 4.1). These five bars form a model that is returned to throughout the movement, each time subjected to modification, as if Hensel is exploring the possibilities of the musical idea or seeking to resolve the issues left open by its initial statement. In order to understand the expressive course of Hensel's opening movement, it is therefore necessary to examine these bars in some detail.

46

Example 4.1 Fanny Hensel, String Quartet (1834), i, opening model

Most notable is the tonal instability of the phrase. E flat major is clearly implied by the opening melodic line, and the harmonies also point initially to this key as the tonic. But no root-position E flat harmony is given (neither for that matter is its dominant reached), and the phrase closes in bar 5 with a perfect authentic cadence (PAC) in the relative C minor. The pivotal stage in this progression is encountered in bar 3. By slipping from E♭ to D in the viola line, Hensel transforms the preceding ii^7 chord to a half-diminished vii^7, which, easily reinterpreted as ii^7 in C minor, is used as a pivot to that key. In fact, this alternative tonal centre has been hinted at right from the start, as the opening harmony is also a C minor chord. Although it is the first sonority heard in the quartet, it is unlikely that any listener would conceive of this harmony as a potential tonic, at least for anything more than a moment: the first two bars outline a familiar vi – I^6– ii$^6_5$ cadential approach in E flat major, in which the C minor chord functions as vi, and the second harmony given in the latter half of bar 1 (a first inversion E♭ chord, with B♭ prominent in two voices) immediately undermines the potential sense of C minor. Still, when the following bars revert to C minor, the initial suggestion becomes in retrospect more than an incidental detail.

The initial tonal problem Hensel sets out reveals how much she conceives her string quartet as being in dialogue with specific earlier works in the genre. Both of Beethoven's quartets in the same key – Opp. 74 and 127 – form an important backdrop to Hensel's piece. Most significant, though, is the relation with her brother's own E flat major Quartet, Op. 12 – a work that responds to these same two Beethoven quartets – which Hensel got to know in September 1829, a few weeks before starting the first version of her movement. Like Beethoven's Op. 74, the opening bar of Mendelssohn's Op. 12 features a prominent flattened leading note, Db, that creates a strong early movement to the subdominant (an inclination also conspicuous across Op. 127). In Mendelssohn's work, however, this is soon extended into a tendency towards the minor mode – C minor and G minor in the introduction, and then at a larger level by F minor (more specifically, the dominant of F minor) in a new, distinctly troubled theme that takes over the first movement's development section. Over the course of the quartet's four movements, the tension between the rival tonal centres and their associated thematic material creates an expressive fissure in the musical argument, culminating in a remarkable off-tonic C minor finale, which only resolves to the overall tonic of E flat major in the coda via the return of the first movement's F minor theme.[1] In her initial equivocation between E flat major and C minor, Hensel is taking up one of the central formal concerns of Mendelssohn's quartet, but now foregrounding it as a compositional problem from the very outset. It is hardly surprising that Mendelssohn would single out this opening 'swaying between E flat and C minor' as one of the features he most liked about his sister's movement.

Hensel's quartet effectively forms 'a musical "answer"', as Bartsch puts it, to her brother's latest work in the genre, which itself responds to Beethoven's later quartets.[2] The relationship between the two is further underscored by numerous thematic links. Aside from the initial rhythmic similarity, as Hellwig-Unruh has pointed out, Hensel's opening melodic line retraces that of the first theme in Mendelssohn's ensuing sonata movement (*Allegro non tardante*): the parallel is clearest in bars 24–5, though these bars modify the opening motive (bb. 18–21), which in turn derives from the Adagio introduction (see Example 4.2(a) and (b)).[3] Moreover, when this material returns in the coda of Mendelssohn's finale (bb. 241–4, Example 4.2(c)) the rhythmic affinity with Hensel's theme is even closer.[4] Hensel's initial vi harmony also reflects the start of her brother's theme in bar 18 (in Mendelssohn's work the C in the bass supports subdominant harmony, a feature which in turn draws from

The Opening Paradigm

Example 4.2 Thematic similarities between (a) Hensel, String Quartet, i, bb. 1–5, (b) Mendelssohn, String Quartet Op. 12, i, bb. 18–25, (c) Mendelssohn, String Quartet Op. 12, iv, bb. 241–4, and (d) Mendelssohn, Overture *Calm Sea and Prosperous Voyage*, Op. 27, bb. 1–2

the link between Maestoso and Allegro at the opening of Beethoven's Op. 127, bb. 5–7). Arguably even more important is the potential allusion to the opening motive of Mendelssohn's *Calm Sea and Prosperous Voyage* Overture (Example 4.2(d)), which Hensel reworks in her opening line.[5] This is a theme that we know held great significance within the family circle at the time: it had become associated with Mendelssohn's own sea voyage to England and his absence overseas in the period Hensel came to write the movement, and the full implications of this thematic correspondence will be taken up later at the end of this chapter.

Hensel's opening thus sets out an initial thematic model or paradigm (what I will label *a*) that will return throughout the movement, each time recontextualised, reharmonised, or otherwise reinterpreted, following intervening material that offers some contrast. Rather than first appearing in its archetypal form and then being subjected to variation, however, it might be more helpful to understand this procedure as occurring in reverse. Compromised at the start by the tonal deflection to C minor, the process of the movement is to search for a more satisfactory resolution to this theme, in which the ideal version cadencing successfully to E flat major will be attained only at the very end. The resulting structure bears little resemblance to established formal models but possesses its own intrinsic logic.

Formal Outline

An overview of the movement is given in Table 4.1 and musically illustrated in Example 4.3. As can be seen, in thematic layout, the movement alternates between the initial idea (*a*) and contrasting material. The resulting design is actually not that dissimilar to a rondo principle in the contrast between a main theme and more episodic passages, though one would hesitate to describe it in these terms given the small scale of the sections and the nature of the material.[6] At the same time, harmonically the movement traces a journey from its initial state of tonal instability towards the final clarification of E flat major.

Following the opening theme's deflection to C minor and the cadence in bar 5, Hensel introduces an imitative passage built on

Table 4.1 *Formal design of Hensel's String Quartet, i*

Bars	Thematic Material	Tonal Areas	Cadences
1–5	a	vi/E♭ – Cm	Cm PAC b. 5
5–13	b	Cm–	
14–20	a′	A♭^{6}–	Fm PAC b. 20
20–7	c	Fm–V/Cm	
28–36	a″+b, d→	Cm^6–Fm^6–	
37–43	d	V/Fm	
44–9	a1	F–B♭–V/E♭	
50–61	c	V/E♭	
62–72	a2, b	V/E♭	
73–7	a	vi/E♭–E♭	E♭ IAC b. 77

a new figure in even crotchets (*b*). This sequence of ideas continues the parallels with the introduction to Mendelssohn's own E flat quartet (bb. 6–9) but also closens the movement's affinities with the contrapuntal opening of Beethoven's Op. 131. Initially oscillating between C minor and its own minor dominant, from bar 10 a second set of entries swings the music towards the subdominant, F minor, but this soon deflects towards its own relative major and brings about a second statement of the opening idea (*a*). Transposed here to A flat, the model is also modified to start on a first-inversion tonic, the third bar being reharmonised to provide a stronger secondary dominant, and the final cadence extended by two bars through repetition. Nevertheless, despite these slight alterations, the underlying progression is the same, moving down a third from A flat to its relative, F minor. As a result, the music has moved away from the ostensible tonic, E flat, in a series of descending thirds via C minor and A flat to F minor.

The cadence at the close of the second iteration of phrase *a* (b. 20) now elides with the next episode (*c*). Again imitative, this material possesses a mild similarity with the preceding *b* episode, though the movement is now quicker, in quavers. Bringing the music back to the dominant of C minor, the passage leads to the third iteration of *a*, given this time over first-inversion C minor harmony (b. 28). From this point on the music becomes

Example 4.3 Schematic overview of thematic ideas in Hensel, String Quartet, i,
and their elaboration

more continuous and developmental in character. Model *a* is combined contrapuntally with *b* in the inner voices, and the phrase is
subjected to fragmentation and sequence. Given successively on

Example 4.3 (cont.)

C minor and F minor, *a* is now shortened to three bars, creating a small-scale effect of acceleration, and cutting across the two-bar hypermetre suggested by the statements of *b* in violin 2 and viola. The latter's tail is diminuted from crotchets to quavers, and from bar 32 it gives way in the second violin to a figure that now suggests *c*. This, in turn, is immediately modified into a new motive (*d*, violin 2 bb. 33–4, violin 1 bb. 35–6) that prefigures the material of the next episode.

Taking up this new motive *d*, the passage at bar 37 forms an extended build-up on the dominant of F minor that resolves in bar 44 to a first-inversion F major chord. The material heard here is derived once more from the main theme, but at this point *a* also proves subject to evolving variation, given in rhythmic diminution and extended through modified repetition, to an extent that warrants treating this idea as a new offshoot of the original (a^1). Crucially, too, the turn to the major mode at this point will allow the music to regain the movement's overall tonic: after the long preceding passage vacillating between C minor and F minor, F major now becomes a dominant leading through the cycle of fifths to B flat (b. 46), and this in turn is transformed into a dominant of E flat (b. 50). This is a highly significant moment of arrival: hitherto the movement's tonic has been absent, but from this point the ensuing music forms a long consolidation of its dominant, leading to the resolution of the final bars.

Although the music still alternates between the opening *a* material and that of the intervening episodes, from here on the two are much more integrated. Thus, the *a*-based passage of bars 44–9 is followed by a passage derived from *c* that consolidates the dominant proposed at bar 50 and leads to a cadential 6/4 in bars 60–2. The ensuing passage (bb. 62–72) reworks the previous variant of *a* into a longer-breathed melodic entity over a dominant pedal (again it is sufficiently distinct to merit labelling a further variant, a^2). The first cadential approach at bar 68 is deflected towards the submediant and motive *b* is now introduced into the bass adding a contrapuntal thickening to the texture. Whether by accident or design, with this motivic recall Hensel completes a near palindromic layout of thematic ideas, a–b–a–c–a (+b)–d–a^1–c–a^2–b–a, in which the long pedal on V/Fm at bar 37 – motive *d* – forms the midpoint of the seventy-seven-bar movement.[7] Yet the continual variation of the opening thematic model *a* over the course of the movement and the increasing integration with the episodic material creates a sense of ongoing process and growth, which culminates in the melodic blossoming of the final section.

The final stage in this process is provided by the return of model *a* in something approaching its original form, which makes up the final five bars of the movement (bb. 73–7). Not only does this statement complete the palindromic symmetry of material presented in the movement, but it also forms the successful end point in the series of reconfigurations of the opening idea. The passage is reached via the interruption of the cadence signalled over bars 72–3. As we saw, the projected cadence a few bars earlier (bb. 68–9) had already been deflected onto the submediant, C minor, through the introduction of motive *b* in the bass at its original pitch level, necessitating a stronger 'one more time' approach in the following bars; but this second attempt at a cadence also proves insufficient. The interrupted cadence now formed links quite naturally into the initial vi harmony of the opening theme. Indeed, in doing so, Hensel finally reveals something of the true nature of this phrase: it is essentially a closing gesture, a cadential phrase, which would be syntactically most appropriate following on as a continuation of preceding music. By using it now not as an initiating gesture but running it on from an interrupted cadence, Hensel at last provides an initial context for the opening submediant harmony – the C minor that proved so off-putting for the tonal course of the movement.

There is a wonderful sense of rediscovery to the re-emergence of this opening theme, of quiet fulfilment of what the music had held out from the beginning but never yet quite attained. And now, after all its different reconfigurations in the intervening music, the opening phrase will at last find its way to the tonic. For the crucial third bar (b. 75), in which the passage had previously slipped to a ii^7 of C minor through lowering the viola's E♭ to D, Hensel instead raises the cello's A♭ to A♮, creating a secondary dominant seventh (F–A–C–E♭) in E flat. With this tiny chromatic alteration, the phrase leads at last to a cadential 6/4 of the movement's long-suppressed tonic, E flat. Indeed, this entire progression had been prefigured a few bars earlier, arising as part of a sequence in bars 56–60. Although the material – an elaboration of *c* – did not obviously relate to model *a*, the harmonic template and bassline matches the final section, revealing how its initial vi–I^6–ii^6 progression may be rationalised within a larger sequence (the series of deceptive V–vi motions over descending third roots creating the Romanesca-style bass of bb. 55–8) and adumbrating the decisive

A♭–A♮–B♭ bassline. There the progression led to the arrival 6/4 at bar 60; here, in the closing bars with the return to theme *a*, the regained 6/4 leads to the dominant and thence, at last, resolves to the tonic.

This is the perfect cadence to E♭ that the movement had been searching for and only now, in the last bar, is finally found. And yet, there is a sense of incompletion, of longing that is still not completely fulfilled. Even at the movement's close, the melodic line remains on the third scale degree, G, rather than finding a resting point on the tonic E flat. This is especially pointed as the preceding melodic line had been strongly indicating such resolution: the second scale degree F had been given twice in bar 74^2 and 75^2, continuing the descent from G as if to reach the tonic in the following bars. But the melodic line in the final two bars rises to $\hat{5}$, echoing the middle part of the opening motive (B♭–A♭–G), and at the end the listener is left with a curious sense of satisfaction at the final arrival of a tonic cadence admixed with incompletion in the melodic voice.[8]

'Innere Nothwendigkeit' and 'Schematic Fantasies'

It is this principle of thematic alternation and variation combined with the exploratory tonal structure that is responsible for the movement's oft-noted fantasia impression. The fact that there is also no clear relation to familiar formal models accentuates the sense that the music is freely formed, obeying the imaginative impulses of its creator rather than a preformed rule or schema.

Felix Mendelssohn, as we saw in the previous chapter, found the result verging on the excessive in its avoidance of the nominal tonic for large parts and cadential concentration on alternative tonal centres of C minor and F minor. Even if it might be justified within the first movement, over the course of all four movements the protracted avoidance of the ostensible tonic detracted from the music's comprehensibility and became in his view a mannerism. In missing a sense of 'inner inevitability' to the tonal structure, her brother's criticism perhaps downplays the logical aspects of Hensel's design, especially the recovery of the tonic through the strongly directed cycle of fifths progression from bar 44.[9] But still it points to Hensel's departure from generic tonal schemes and likely expectations on the part of listeners. It is hardly to be foreseen that a movement ostensibly 'in' E flat major – governed by an E flat tonic – will spend much of its duration wavering between C minor and F minor before the nominal tonic has even been articulated: these vacillations could neither be predicted in advance, nor in themselves establish any clear alternative pattern (at least up to b. 44, before the cycle of fifths comes into play).[10]

Yet as we have seen, there is also a compelling logic to Hensel's design, albeit one that bears little resemblance to generically customary formal layouts. The movement is constructed from the continual reworking of its initial five-bar thematic model, a 'paradigmatic' approach to composition whereby the different implications of a given musical phrase are worked through over the course of the piece. This quality surely points to Hensel's strong grounding in earlier eighteenth-century compositional practice – as exemplified for instance in the music of J. S. Bach – as well as suggesting comparison with the use of tonal schemata recently identified in much later eighteenth-century music.[11] Moreover, the order of these statements is controlled to create at the largest scale an arc of tension and resolution, while the intervening material of the episodes follows a symmetrical layout and also takes part in the process of development. Hensel's design follows a clear inner logic without necessarily appearing inevitable in its course of events: in this, she adopts a more intuitive, 'fantasia'-like approach than her brother's dialogic orientation towards generic expectations. And even her fantasy follows patterns.

In a recent article, Stephen Rodgers has identified the same fantasia quality in several of Hensel's songs and offered an important basis for a more thorough analytical account of her musical language.[12] As Rodgers notes, 'The idea that Hensel's music engages in fantasy has become a persistent refrain in the reception of her work.'[13] However, he contends, 'analysis reveals that many of Hensel's most fantasy-like passages result less from experimentation *outside* structural archetypes than from experimentation *with* structural archetypes – archetypes that she manipulates in order to create the *effect* of fantasy'. Rodgers focusses on 'two recurring archetypes or "personal schemata" that involve the avoidance or abandonment of the tonic in the very opening phrases of a piece', what he describes as 'tonal deflections'.[14] Her songs, he points out, 'often abandon their home keys very quickly, as if on a whim, returning to the tonic only at the end of a section, or the end of an entire piece'. Closer inspection nevertheless reveals that Hensel 'often modulates to the same keys, and in the same ways. The two key areas she overwhelmingly favors, when starting in the major mode, are vi and ii.'[15]

Rodgers does not apply this analysis to Hensel's instrumental music, although he notes in passing Todd's description of the quartet's opening movement as a 'free, formally diffuse movement that resembles a fantasia'.[16] But almost everything I have quoted above could have been expressly written of the quartet's Adagio. The initial deflection from the tonic, E flat, and the postponement of its confirmation until the very last bar of the movement are the same as that which Rodgers identifies in Hensel's songs, as is the strong predilection for vi and ii key areas – C minor and F minor in its E flat major context. In fact, the opening thematic model (*a*) is an elaborated version of what Rodgers calls the 'submediant schema', one of Hensel's favourite opening gambits. In this melodic-contrapuntal pattern, the bass voice descends from the tonic to scale-degree 4, which is reinterpreted as an upper neighbour to the dominant of the submediant (see Figure 4.21a). The quartet's opening essentially follows this plan but offers a more elaborate initial stage, in which the tonic is already destabilised by beginning on vi before moving to a weaker first inversion (Figure 4.1b; given the mirror-image presentation of thematic ideas over the movement, it is curious to note the palindromic aspect of the progression, clearest in the bass line). The result is that Hensel's piece appears to be starting *in medias res*, in the midst of a cadential approach, which itself is deflected to a wrong tonal outcome and remains unresolved until the final bars of the movement.

At a larger level, too, Rodgers identifies a characteristic pattern in his analysis of a pair of Hensel's songs that corresponds quite closely to the broader trajectory of the quartet's opening movement. In Rodgers's model, each song proceeds in four stages: '(1) a move

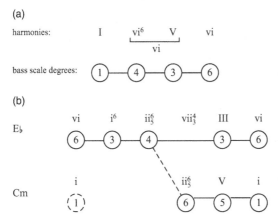

Figure 4.1a Rodgers's 'Submediant Schema' for Hensel's songs
Figure 4.1b Elaboration of the 'Submediant Schema' at the opening of
Hensel's Quartet

to ii, (2) a move to vi, (3) a tonal excursion that heads into more distant realms, and (4) a return to the home key and a structural perfect authentic cadence'.[17] The quartet varies this outline slightly, but the common features can nonetheless still be seen. At the largest level, the movement deflects away from the implied tonic at the opening towards C minor and F minor areas (A flat also briefly appears between the two, though is less prominent and serves as the relative to F minor). Over half the movement is spent alternating between vi and ii areas, before a large-scale progression moves back through the cycle of fifths to reach the dominant of the home key of E flat, whose tonic is secured in the last bar (here with a weaker imperfect authentic cadence, though this is still the only cadence to the tonic in the entire movement). Moreover, as Todd notes, by initially moving down from the tonic through thirds (E♭–Cm–A♭–Fm) and then rising back up through fourths (Cm–Fm–B♭–E♭), Hensel creates a quasi-symmetrical logic.[18]

Although there is no straightforward relation with a generic formal schema, some writers on the quartet have nevertheless proposed ingenious variations on more familiar layouts. In his brief account of the movement, for instance, Todd has suggested

59

that the movement's structure may be considered akin to a sonata form, but with its initial section, the exposition, missing, and which therefore starts in the midst of a development section. Given the caveats that must be made in order to accommodate the movement to any idea of sonata design, the need for the parallel may seem a little strained.[19] But in identifying the developmental tendency of much of the music, Todd has his finger on the cause of its fantasia quality, as well as the curious sense that the attainment of the tonic at the end of the piece is in a sense a recovery or return to origins, despite the fact that this has never been fully present before.

Hensel's Adagio thus searches for its tonic throughout, replacing the customary three-part stability–instability–stability pattern of the eighteenth-century sonata with her own progressive paradigm, in which a destabilised opening is the start of a long journey of recovery. As Todd discerns, the result is a movement from instability to stability – a much more 'Romantic' structure, where the final resolution occurs only in the very last bar.[20] In some ways, then, Mendelssohn was right: the earlier parts of the movement are 'not in a key at all', if by key [*Tonart*] we look for an articulated sense of the overriding tonic, E flat. But Hensel often seems more concerned with *searching* for a key, a quite different aesthetic precept resulting in quite different tonal structures.

Musical Correspondences and Meaning

In an earlier article on 'Fanny Hensel's Lied Aesthetic', Stephen Rodgers has pointed to the frequent absence of tonics in her songs as 'emblems of loss and desire'. 'Arguably, the surest sign of Hensel's Lied aesthetic is her tendency to undermine the stability of the tonic', he writes – to evade it repeatedly throughout so that its final return 'at the end of a song or a larger formal section aligns with the end of a thought, or the revelation of an idea'.[21] 'These absent tonics are emblems of loss and desire, signs of needs unfulfilled, hopes dashed, emotions unsettled.'[22] In a song such as the Heine setting 'Verlust' (written in 1827 and published in her brother's Op. 9 collection), 'the music searches for closure as the poetic persona searches for comfort'.[23] Such a search for a stable tonic, a resting point or 'home', is of course equally the process of the quartet's opening Adagio. And it is here that the idea of music as correspondence, as a form of intimate communication, becomes especially relevant for interpreting the movement. In seeking to understand the expressive meaning of Hensel's idiosyncratic formal design, it is useful to consider once again the allusions to her brother's music that are found within it.

Already in her C minor Piano Sonata of 1823 and in the *Liederkreis* of 1829, Hensel had turned to music as a means of filling distance, composing these pieces 'for Felix, in his absence'. Both works allude to her brother's own compositions, refashioning a characteristic melodic phrase to establish a communicative link with her absent sibling in the manner so well described by Cornelia Bartsch under the rubric of 'music as correspondence'. A similar situation, I propose, surely applies in the case of the opening movement of the quartet, originally written just a few months after the *Liederkreis* as the opening of the unfinished piano sonata, at a time when Mendelssohn was still absent in England, kept away from the family home and his sister's wedding. By her own account, this specific turn from texted song to instrumental music was attractive for Hensel in providing a more 'discreet' medium for expressing her thoughts and feelings at this time.[24] And in the Adagio she subsequently wrote, it is not only the interaction with Mendelssohn's newly completed string quartet in the same key, but especially the opening allusion to his overture of the previous year, *Calm Sea and Prosperous Voyage*, that is crucial to take into account.

There is ample evidence that the overture, and especially the main theme, possessed special significance for the Mendelssohn family circle. In January 1829, a few months before Felix was due to depart for England, he and Fanny played the overture as a piano duet at home with dimmed lighting, upsetting Fanny, for whom his imminent departure was hard to bear: 'the evening was particularly painful' she confided to her diary, 'and the parting and separation moved my soul deeply'.[25] A couple of months later, writing back to his family having crossed the Channel, Felix cursed his choice of poetic subject in the overture: the crossing had been far from smooth, making a mockery of the ostensible tranquillity of Goethe's sea voyage.[26] In turn, in her first letter to him in London, Fanny greeted him by invoking the three trumpets that herald the arrival in port at the end of the overture: this is indeed the same motive that Wilhelm would depict visually on the score of her *Liederkreis* that summer.[27] Moreover, on his return Felix would reference in his own music the overture's opening motive in a semi-autobiographical manner: in the sixth song from the joint Op. 9 collection, 'Scheidend (Auf der Fahrt)' (Parting (On the Voyage)), the male persona departs from the land of his youth to the *Calm Sea* theme, heard in the depths of the bass in the first bar.[28] Thus the overture – and especially the opening motive – threads its way through the family's music, letters, and even visual images of this time, serving as a symbol of Felix Mendelssohn's adventures overseas and his keenly felt absence at home.[29]

Given this context – the precedent for corresponding with her absent brother through musical allusion to his work and the clear private meaning attached to the phrase from *Calm Sea* within the family circle – it is hard to believe that Hensel's Adagio was not conceived, in part, as expressing a similar personal message. The process of the quartet's opening movement, as we have seen, is to offer a search for completion to the opening *Calm Sea* motive, a homecoming to the tonic key that is held out as a possibility in the first bars but eludes closure until the very end, after a long and winding journey through distant tonal reaches. On a musical and expressive level, the movement is 'about' these very same themes: departure, absence, the longing for a point of rest that is continually frustrated, which is finally but only provisionally attained in the final bars. Although it is not necessary to understand this biographical background in order to appreciate the skill and expressive beauty of Hensel's movement, the private connotations correspond perfectly to the musical processes; knowing them adds a layer of richness to our understanding of the music.

The metaphor of the voyage is singularly appropriate, Michael Steinberg holds, for understanding the journey through life of both Mendelssohn siblings.[30] A voyage is what Hensel articulates in musical and connotative terms in the opening movement of her quartet, a search for a fitting close, for a stable 'home' or point of rest. The irony, of course, given her brother's subsequent critical reaction to its wandering tonal structure, is that Hensel's movement is in a sense 'about' him: a 'musical answer' to his own recent quartet in the same key, a response to a favourite orchestral work of his, and most intimately, an expression of his sister's wish to be reunited with him once more.

Notes

1. See the more extensive analysis in Benedict Taylor, *Mendelssohn, Time and Memory: The Romantic Conception of Cyclic Form* (Cambridge: Cambridge University Press, 2011), pp. 170–208.
2. Cornelia Bartsch, 'Fanny Hensels einziges Streichquartett – ein Problemfall? Fanny Hensels Streichquartett zwischen Zuweisungen und Aneignung', in Claudia von Braunmühl (ed.), *Etablierte Wissenschaft und feministische Theorie im Dialog* (Berlin: Berliner Wissenschafts-Verlag, 2003), pp. 135–58, at p. 142. Or as she puts it elsewhere, the quartet 'is to be understood as a personal "answer" to her brother's grappling with Beethoven' (Bartsch, *Fanny Hensel, geb. Mendelssohn: Musik als Korrespondenz* (Kassel: Furore, 2007), p. 305).
3. Hellwig-Unruh, 'Zur Entstehung von Fanny Hensels Streichquartett', p. 139. As opposed to Op. 127, Beethoven's Op. 74 does not really constitute a 'late work', though; it sits between the customary 'middle' and 'late' periods.
4. See Bartsch, *Musik als Korrespondenz*, p. 328.
5. R. Larry Todd, *Fanny Hensel: The Other Mendelssohn* (New York: Oxford University Press, 2010), p. 184.
6. Victoria Sirota likewise remarks on this rondo aspect ('The Life and Works of Fanny Mendelssohn Hensel', DMA diss., Boston University, 1981, p. 240).
7. A slightly diverging reading of the movement's symmetrical layout is given by Annegret Huber, 'Zerschlagen, zerfließen oder erzeugen? Fanny Hensel und Felix Mendelssohn im Streit um musikalische Formkonzepte nach "Beethovens letzter Zeit"', in Betina Brand and Martina Helmig (eds.), *Maßstab Beethoven? Komponistinnen im Schatten des Geniekults* (Munich: edition text+kritik, 2001), pp. 120–44 at 136–7.
8. This is another feature that takes further a quality of Mendelssohn's Op. 12. Mendelssohn's first movement exposition ends similarly with an IAC closing the opening theme with $\hat{3}$ uppermost, and while the upper voice at the end of the movement rises to a tonic E♭, the melodic close has been on G.

9. Here it may be more helpful to think of Mendelssohn's 'innere Nothwendigkeit' as signifying something more like inner 'inevitability' rather than 'necessity'. For him, one can infer, the tonal design, for maximal clarity, demands to be heard against customary tonal schemes and expectations – not, it must be emphasised, necessarily conforming to them, but nevertheless positing them as the point of reference, against which departures can be understood as expressive demands arising from the nature of the material. Hensel, writing for herself, makes no such concessions to ease of comprehensibility.

10. I am grateful to Thomas Schmidt for suggesting this interpretation.

11. On eighteenth-century tonal schemata see particularly Robert O. Gjerdingen, *Music in the Galant Style* (New York: Oxford University Press, 2007).

12. Stephen Rodgers, 'Fanny Hensel's Schematic Fantasies: or, The Art of Beginning', in Laurel Parsons and Brenda Ravenscroft (eds.), *Analytical Essays on Music by Women Composers* (New York: Oxford University Press, 2018), pp. 151–74.

13. Ibid., p. 151.

14. Ibid., p. 152.

15. Ibid., p. 153.

16. Todd, *Fanny Hensel*, p. 181, cited in Rodgers, 'Fanny Hensel's Schematic Fantasies', p. 171 n. 2.

17. Rodgers, 'Fanny Hensel's Schematic Fantasies', p. 156.

18. Todd, *Fanny Hensel*, p. 181.

19. Todd speaks of 'a foreshortened sonata-form movement that commences in the middle of the process', with 'a recapitulation of material implied, not previously heard'; ibid., pp. 138, 182. Beyond the conceptual difficulty of a reprise of unheard material, it is hard to see where the recapitulation would start; the first possible location would be bar 62, though the material at this point is presented over a continuation of the preceding dominant pedal and is surely heard as composing out the cadential 6/4, that is, as a postponement of the impending cadence, joined to and an outgrowth of the previous section, and not as a new beginning. It is also hard for me to discern any qualities in the remaining passage of music that could reliably indicate it belonged to an exposition.

20. Charles Rosen, for instance, has identified this pattern as lying at the heart of the un-classical, 'Romantic' formal dynamic of Robert Schumann's *Fantasie* in C, Op. 17, a piece composed a few years later, in 1836–8 (see Rosen, *The Classical Style: Haydn, Mozart, Beethoven* (London: Faber, 1971), pp. 451–2).

21. Rodgers, 'Fanny Hensel's Lied Aesthetic', *Journal of Musicological Research*, 30 (2011), 175–201, at p. 186.

22. Ibid., p. 188.
23. Ibid., p. 187.
24. See the letter to Wilhelm Hensel, *c.* mid-September 1829, in Martina Helmig and Annette Maurer (eds.), 'Fanny Mendelssohn Bartholdy und Wilhelm Hensel: Briefe aus der Verlobungszeit', in Martina Helmig (ed.), *Fanny Hensel, geb. Mendelssohn Bartholdy: Das Werk* (Munich: edition text+kritik, 1997), p. 155.
25. Entry for 8 January 1829, in *Fanny Hensel: Tagebücher*, ed. Hans-Günter Klein and Rudolf Elvers (Wiesbaden: Breitkopf & Härtel, 2002), p. 2. ('es war mir den Abend ganz besonders wehmüthig, und die Trennung und das Entbehren mir sehr nah vor die Seele gerückt.')
26. Mendelssohn, letter from London, 21 April 1829, in *Sämtliche Briefe*, ed. Helmut Loos, Wilhelm Seidel, et al., 12 vols. (Kassel: Bärenreiter, 2008–17), vol. I, p. 267.
27. Hensel, letter of 18 April 1829, in Marcia Citron, *The Letters of Fanny Hensel to Felix Mendelssohn, Collected, Edited and Translated with Introductory Essays and Notes* (Stuyvesant, NY: Pendragon, 1987), p. 23 (English translation)/p. 385 (German original).
28. Todd, *Fanny Hensel*, p. 143. The text is either by Droysen or Mendelssohn himself; the musical autograph for the song is dated 13 January 1830, a month after Mendelssohn's return.
29. Motives like this could also operate humorously within the close Mendelssohn circle. Gustav Droysen's son relates that the 'cello theme' from *Calm Sea* was also Droysen's 'welcome music' (*Begrüßungssignal*) in the Mendelssohn household; it is not clear from the description, though, whether this was the opening of the overture or the second subject that is derived from it. See Gustav Droysen, 'Johann Gustav Droysen und Felix Mendelssohn-Bartholdy', *Deutsche Rundschau*, 111 (1902), 116; quoted by Celia Applegate in 'Mendelssohn and Droysen: Historicism in Practice and Theory', in Benedict Taylor (ed.), *Rethinking Mendelssohn* (New York: Oxford University Press, 2020), pp. 158–82 at 160. Todd also suggests the influence of Mendelssohn's overture on two of Hensel's later orchestral works from 1832, the dramatic *scena Hero und Leander* (H-U262) and the Overture in C major (H-U265); *Fanny Hensel*, pp. 161 and 163.
30. Michael P. Steinberg, 'Introduction: Culture, Gender, and Music: A Forum on the Mendelssohn Family', *Musical Quarterly*, 77 (1993), 649.

5

SECOND MOVEMENT

Allegretto

Hensel's second movement is a scherzo in all but name. In fact, as we saw in Chapter 3, the earliest sketch for the material is designated 'scherzo', and in their correspondence both Hensel and Mendelssohn refer to the completed movement as a scherzo, so it seems justifiable to describe it openly in these terms. In following her opening movement with this Allegretto, Hensel is firmly putting paid to any lingering expectations that the Adagio would serve as an introduction to a sonata-form first movement: retrospectively, at least, it clearly constitutes a movement in its own right.

As was also noted, the first version of the movement, the 'intermezzo' from the unfinished piano sonata of 1829, consisted only of the opening section (bb. 1–53). In transforming the piece into a quartet in 1834, Hensel added the extensive central section (bb. 53–143) before bringing back a truncated version of the opening material to create a ternary scherzo-and-trio design. However, there are some complications over alterations entered into the autograph score which impact the conception of the scherzo and need to be clarified before any further discussion of the movement.

Larger Design, Difficulties with Sources, and the Two Versions

In no other movement are autograph source issues so pressing as in this scherzo. As we know from her letter to Mendelssohn of 4 November 1834, Hensel had revised the movement following her brother's feedback, and it is quite probably these changes that are transmitted in the numerous pastings-over and even an entire replacement page in the autograph (the only complete source we have for the quartet; see Figure 5.1 for an example of the

Figure 5.1 Hensel, String Quartet (1834), ii, page from first version (A), showing passages of the trio subsequently pasted over with snippets of scherzo material. Staatsbibliothek zu Berlin – Preußischer Kulturbesitz, Berlin, MA Ms. 43, 16 [11]

67

manuscript). These reveal a shift between two quite different formal conceptions of the movement. In the first (A), still easily reconstructed from under the pasted-over bars and discarded page, the opening C minor scherzo was followed by the fugal trio starting in C major, leading to a compressed reprise of the scherzo whose latter part is truncated and dissolves into the movement's closing bars. This might sound like the version known now, but the revision is actually rather more subtle and blurs the clear boundary between internal trio and scherzo reprise. In this second version (B), two-bar snippets of the scherzo's opening phrase are already introduced from bar 101 onwards amidst the latter part of the trio. Heard four times (at bb. 101, 105, 114, and 118), they eventually lead to what might seem a retransition drawing on the scherzo's continuation (b. 133), but rather than resulting in the return of the scherzo's opening and a clear sense of ternary reprise, the preparatory dominant of bb. 140–3 elides with the scherzo's continuation phrase from bar 9. In effect, the fragments of scherzo material heard from bar 101 are not preparatory but actually constitute the point of thematic return (to the extent there is one), which is slyly intercut between the climactic phrases of the trio.

The major difficulty facing the innocent performer, listener, or student is that the more widely used edition of the quartet, that edited by Günter Marx and issued by Breitkopf und Härtel, incorrectly prints alternative passages from the first and second versions adjacently at this point, creating a form of the movement that Hensel never wrote and which gives a misleading idea of quite how radical her conception is. (Renate Eggebrecht-Kupsa's later edition for Furore accurately transmits the revised version, though most subsequent performers have tended to use the Breitkopf und Härtel edition.[1]) The sticking point is bars 144–51 in the Breitkopf und Härtel edition, which form the start of the scherzo's ternary reprise. These eight bars, however, are an editorial revision of four bars (with repeat signs, possibly added at an intermediate stage)[2] that belong to the earlier version and are either pasted over or crossed through in Hensel's autograph (see Example 5.1).[3]

The material which replaced it in the autograph is part of the preceding retransition, which was not present in the original version, but in the Breitkopf edition directly precedes this reprise.

Example 5.1 Hensel, String Quartet, ii, retransition and elided reprise, original version

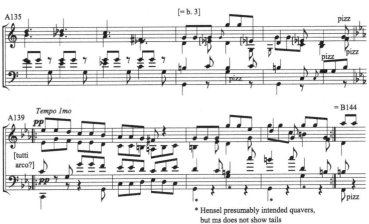

* Hensel presumably intended quavers,
but ms does not show tails

Although a note is given to an 'alternative version' in the critical report at the end (given in German only), the form of the movement that is printed is something that Hensel never wrote and simply an editorial creation, running two mutually exclusive passages – an original and its replacement – one after the other.[4] This intervention creates a more normal reprise; it undercuts quite how radical Hensel's curtailment of the expected scherzo reprise is and diminishes the significance of the preceding fragments of scherzo material that Hensel has inserted in her revisions into the latter stages of the trio. In the final, second version of the movement, rather than a clear-cut point of reprise (that the conflated Breitkopf edition suggests has been fitfully foreshadowed in the trio), Hensel diffuses the reprise function over the second part of the movement, intercutting both types of material – trio and scherzo – to create a remarkable effect of two parallel streams ongoing simultaneously. In light of the already highly compressed return of scherzo material and the tonal instability of the final bars (see pp. 74–6 below), the result is a movement that increasingly dissolves formal and tonal modes of articulation, slowly unravelling as it approaches its end.

Whether or not Hensel's brother was partly responsible for this new formal conception is uncertain. On the one hand, such dissolution is typical of Hensel's own, quite individual approach to tonality and form, one which her brother found too unclear for his own taste: the effect is undeniably far more 'Henselian' than 'Mendelssohnian'. On the other, we have her own word that she revised the movement on his advice, and revisions – whether those made in response to Mendelssohn's comments or entered independently at some other time – are clearly transmitted in the autograph. And Mendelssohn's own scherzi contain no less radical or outrageous formal ploys – just rarely do they take this specific form.[5] It is probably impossible to prove either way, though one suspects the formal deftness is something her brother would at least have appreciated, even if the tonal instability might have been a step too far for him. Hensel's intercutting of scherzo and trio recalls something of the finale of Mendelssohn's earlier Octet (a work also in E flat), whose finale (the opening fugato of which is not miles away from Hensel's trio) brings back snippets of the preceding scherzo in a comparable manner, while the drastic curtailment of the reprise is also paralleled in the cuts Mendelssohn made to that work's second movement (likewise in C minor) in the early 1830s, whose recapitulation entirely omits the primary theme that had still been present in the original 1825 version. Similarly, the equivocation between C as a tonic and as V/F minor at the end of Hensel's movement directly echoes that at the end of Mendelssohn's *Andante*. None of this is to say that Mendelssohn would have written a scherzo quite like this: the result is distinctly and characteristically Henselian. Here again, we encounter an instance of common practice in which there is nonetheless clear difference between sister and brother in their individual realisation.

Opening Scherzo

The origins of the allegretto's material go back to a sketch from 9 May 1829, which as Annette Nubbemeyer has shown echoes the 'Campanella' Rondo from Paganini's Violin Concerto No. 2 in B minor, Op. 7, a work that Hensel had heard Paganini play just one week earlier at a private concert in Berlin.[6] This four-bar sketch was worked into the primary idea of the 'intermezzo' of the unfinished piano sonata that autumn. It may well simply be

Opening Scherzo

Example 5.2 Hensel, String Quartet, ii, opening idea

coincidence, but in light of the later links between material from different movements it is worth observing that the Paganini-inspired idea fits the new multi-movement context quite neatly: the melodic line retraces the contour and pitches of the Adagio's opening idea, descending from E♭ to F – the latter now sharpened, and with the initial fourth between E♭ and B♭ filled out (see Example 5.2).

Although the construction of this first scherzo section seems unremarkable enough, even here Hensel's propensity for free elaboration of her material is apparent. A scherzo or equivalent dance-like movement would generally be expected to take the form of a rounded binary design at this time (|: a :||: b a' :| or, written out, a a b a' b a'); failing that, some related type of quatrain form (a a b a') might be expected. Hensel initially points in this direction, but the return of her opening phrase becomes much more elaborate, with the result that the second part proves significantly more extensive than might initially have seemed to be the case. Bars 1–4 present the main idea of the section (as illustrated in Example 5.2) – a capricious two-bar idea in 6/8 time whose staggered entries in the lower voices create an imitative effect, followed by two bars prolonging the dominant. This unit is immediately repeated in the following four bars, before a contrasting four-bar idea (b) leads from the dominant back to the tonic through fanning out in the outer voices (bb. 9–12). However, the immediate sequential repetition of this passage, starting now on C, draws the music towards the subdominant, and the *forte* reprise of a section in F minor midway through bar 15 (the loudest dynamic marking yet) proves a false start, corrected two bars later with the true return of this material in the tonic (b. 18).

At this stage we appear to be in the reprise of a small-scale rounded binary or quatrain form. But the returning a' unit is slightly altered and expanded from its initial four bars to ten by the interpolation of a new six-bar segment (bb. 20–5) that effectively prolongs the dominant, in this linking up with the contrasting idea. A further reprise of the phrase is offered at bar 28, corresponding more closely to its original form, but this ends on the dominant once more, leading to yet another attempt (b. 32). This time the phrase is subject to sequential expansion and seems to be setting up a drive to a cadence, but at bar 38 falls back into the music of the interpolation of bars 20–5. Eventually the dominant resolves to the tonic through the descending bass in bars 44–5 (calling to mind the bassline of the b section from bb. 9–12, which has otherwise not been heard in the reprise), but the stepwise descent in the bass diffuses any potency of the long preceding dominant. The following bars simply reiterate the chromatic descent over a tonic pedal, effectively liquidating the thematic material of the section over a long prolongation of C that emphasises the subdominant as much as the tonic. At the end of the section, there is a curious sense that the music has turned round and round on itself before dissipating; any cadential drive has been thoroughly undercut.

Trio

The C major trio that breaks in forthwith, overlapping with the final chord of the opening scherzo section, is organised initially as a loose fugue and reinjects a sense of purpose to proceedings (see Example 5.3). The key, location, and tone of the passage call to mind the comically ungainly fugal trio from the third movement of Beethoven Fifth Symphony, another work in C minor. The four successive entries alternate between tonic and dominant degrees, though there is no strict counter-subject employed, and after a brief stretto in bars 65–7 the music gives way to a free expansion of the material with brief imitative passages. Driven by the continuous stream of rhythmic movement (semiquavers predominate

Example 5.3 Hensel, String Quartet, ii, fugal trio theme

in nearly every bar), the section passes through a variety of keys, to an extent that may disorientate the listener (Mendelssohn, typically, found it too much).

Although there is no single harmonic plan discernible for the entire section, D minor is reached at an early stage (b. 73) and returned to at bar 101 following an intervening journey that has touched on related tonal areas (Gm, B♭, Am) and a rising progression of diminished seventh harmonies (whose texture recalls the scherzo from Mendelssohn's Quintet, Op. 18). At this point (in the revised version) the first quotation of the scherzo breaks in for two-and-a-half bars, initiating a rising sequence interleaving the material of trio and scherzo and moving through E minor to F sharp minor (b. 109), which is held for some time.[7] Significantly, this is the key farthest removed from the C major of the trio's opening, and the *fortissimo* dynamic here is the loudest marking in the movement. Thereafter the music falls through a series of fifths F♯m–Bm–Em–Am (bb. 120–4), generating a second *fortissimo* climax, this time on F major harmony (b. 126). This is the terminal point of the process, however: F major proves rather closer to the trio's initial tonic and now easily becomes contextualised as a subdominant, leading to the dominant G in bar 130 and with it the start of the retransition. From bar 133, scherzo material is brought back, but now more extensively and without any further interjecting remnants of the trio, preparing the seemingly imminent reprise. Bars 136–43 rework bars 38–43, the passage that formed the long dominant near the end of the opening section, which is aptly recontextualised here as a retransition.

Dissolving Reprise

As we have seen, though, the heralded return of the scherzo does not proceed as expected. In revising the movement, Hensel deleted an initial reprise of the scherzo's opening idea (a) and cut straight to the scherzo's continuation phrase (b), first heard at bar 9. The result is an undermining of clear formal articulation at this point, a blurring of trio and scherzo (whose material has already been present for some bars) and the first stage in what will prove a gradual dissolution of the movement's material in the remaining bars.

The logic behind this omission is nevertheless persuasive. The opening scherzo had already presented this phrase multiple times, not just twice at its start, but then three times in its internal reprise from bar 18 (four times if one counts the false reprise in the immediately preceding bars). If the first scherzo section had tended to overuse this material, now the larger movement reprise seeks to redress this imbalance by omitting it entirely. What is more, the opening phrase had also been heard several further times in the trio (bb. 101, 105, 114, 118) and is alluded to once more in modified form at the start of the retransition (bb. 133–5). As I have suggested, these 'preparatory' reprises might retrospectively become understood as substituting for the absence of a full reprise later. All are off-tonic, so from this perspective it is hard to argue that a proper reprise has actually been strewn in pieces over the preceding forty bars. But when after bar 144 the music moves into the continuation of this material, there is nevertheless a strong sense that we have joined the scherzo mid-flow, and the previous fragments of its opening retrospectively join up to form the necessary antecedent to the continuation now heard. Hence, there is a curious effect of two parallel streams of music, for a while ongoing simultaneously, before the scherzo pushes itself to the fore once again. Such intercutting of material is quite remarkable for a work of 1834: Hensel extends some of the cyclic processes seen in her brother's earlier cyclic instrumental works (such as the finales of the Octet or A minor String Quartet, Op. 13), but employs them for material within a movement rather than at a multi-movement level.

Despite joining the scherzo at the equivalent of bar 9, little of the previous section actually returns: not only is the opening cut, but the rest of the scherzo material is also quite drastically truncated. This time the four-bar *b* segment leads to a modified sequential treatment a fifth higher, thus leading to the dominant (bb. 148–51), and continues in the direction of the secondary dominant, which resolves to the tonic C minor simply through the rising chromatic bass. Following eight bars of shifting chromatic lines over a tonic pedal, the final eight bars liquidate the opening idea into a decoration of simple C major harmony. Remarkably, there is no cadence to the tonic anywhere in this final section of the movement. Instead, the long C pedal stretching from bar 158 to the end is reached through the linear progression in the bass, and closure is reinforced through what theorists would term 'prolongational' means, that is, by duration rather than by means of a harmonic progression. Given that the earlier dominant at the end of the retransition does not resolve directly to the tonic either, there is a real lack of tonal stability in the latter part of the movement.[8] At the very end, indeed, the music's repeated plagal progressions seem to equivocate between C as tonic in its own right and its function as the dominant of F minor.

This oscillation between tonic major and subdominant minor at the close is a familiar feature of earlier pieces that may well have served as models for Hensel, such as the closing bars of Beethoven's C sharp minor Quartet, Op. 131, the first movement of the Piano Sonata in C minor, Op. 111, or most pertinently the C minor second movement of Mendelssohn's Octet. Still, in conjunction with the prolongational closure of the preceding bars the result is an undermining of the idea of cadential closure that is one of Hensel's most characteristic compositional traits. Both Stephen Rodgers and Tyler Osborne have recently called attention to such use of 'prolongational closure' in Hensel's music, her unusual use of plagal cadences and tendency to pair tonic and subdominant keys.[9] Though restricted to Hensel's lieder, their reading finds an ideal exemplification at the close of this instrumental movement. And this same ambiguity between a harmony serving as tonic and as the dominant of the subdominant will be taken up from the start of the following movement.

Notes

1. Recordings by Eggebrecht-Kupsa's Fanny Mendelssohn Quartet and the Merel Quartet are rare exceptions. A particularly curious case is a performance by the Attacca Quartet from 2014 on YouTube, who seem to be playing from the original manuscript with minimal editorial interpretation. Seemingly unaware of the alterations and the telltale glue marks on the discarded page of the first version (which pasted it to the blank verso side of the inserted sheet of manuscript paper, now paginated as 13), they simply play the discarded page [12] followed by the replacement [14], with the result that there is an abrupt shift from V/Cm to V/Bm over the join, and a duplication of much of the material that has just been heard as retransition. See https://www.youtube.com/watch?v=4dZeQA8hbkI. More remarkable still is their version of the third movement, which offers both endings, one after the other.

2. The repeat marks are squeezed between notes, giving the impression of having been written into the score afterwards (this is particularly apparent in the violins at the end of the four bars in question, A:142, while the second of the double barlines here was also clearly written at a different stage). It would also be unusual to employ repeat signs for an internal repetition of this brevity. Repeating the entire opening eight bars furthermore diminishes the potential sectional overlap of the last two bars of retransition (A:137–8, which correspond to bb. 3–4 of the original theme, the ostensible reprise at A:139 effectively taking up the material from b. 5).

3. Thus bars 148–50 are pasted over, and bar 151 is crossed through. However, even these are not an accurate transcription of Hensel's score (which omits grace notes at this point and shows some variance in the inner parts). It seems that the editor picked up on the cue for a reprise in Hensel's original version and fashioned a more regular reprise of eight bars taken wholesale from the start of the movement. Marx justifies his intervention by the claim that a 'da capo without bb. 144–51 appears extremely unlikely' – but this is manifestly just what the autograph shows. Moreover, comparison with Hensel's practice in the quartet's two following movements – or indeed in many other pieces, such as the *Easter Sonata* – reveals that the

overlapping, truncation, or blurring of the reprise is highly character-istic of her compositional style. Marx also proposes that the pizzicato instruction for the viola in bar 156 is 'completely incomprehensible without the pasted over "arco" in b. 144', but in fact there is no 'arco' given by Hensel for the viola part there, and emendation of the pizzicato/arco instructions at this point are needed in any version created. In following Hensel's movement from the Breitkopf score, the reader should hence ignore bars 144–51 and continue from bar 152, which should actually be numbered bar 144.

4. These failings in Marx's edition were also noted earlier by Annegret Huber, 'Zerschlagen, zerfließen oder erzeugen? Fanny Hensel und Felix Mendelssohn im Streit um musikalische Formkonzepte nach "Beethovens letzter Zeit"', in Betina Brand and Martina Helmig (eds.), *Maßstab Beethoven? Komponistinnen im Schatten des Geniekults* (Munich: edition text+kritik, 2001), 133, and following her, Cornelia Bartsch, *Fanny Hensel, geb. Mendelssohn: Musik als Korrespondenz* (Kassel: Furore, 2007), p. 320, n. 133. Still, it appears few performers or anglophone com-mentators are aware of this significant shortcoming (it is not even mentioned, for instance, in the review of this edition in *Notes*).

5. Unlike Hensel, Mendelssohn's scherzi often play against sonata expect-ations. See for instance the scherzi of the Octet, Quintet Op. 18, Quartets Op. 44 Nos. 2 and 3, and Piano Trios Nos. 1 and 2. I discuss several of these in 'Formal Jests: The Sonata-Form Scherzo in Mendelssohn's Mature Chamber Music', *Music Analysis*, 40/3 (2021), 451–501; also see Greg Vitercik, 'Mendelssohn the Progressive', *The Journal of Musicological Research*, 8 (1989), 333–74.

6. Annette Nubbemeyer, 'Die Klaviersonaten Fanny Hensels. Analytische Betrachtungen', in Beatrix Borchard and Monika Schwarz-Danuser (eds.), *Fanny Hensel geb. Mendelssohn Bartholdy: Komponieren zwischen Geselligkeitsideal und romantischer Musikästhetik* (Stuttgart: J. B. Metzler, 1999), pp. 102–4.

7. The same harmonic scheme is present in the earlier version of the movement: in making her revisions, Hensel has by and large replaced two-bar segments of trio-derived *Fortspinnung* with more character-istic scherzo material. The slight exceptions are bars 118–19 in the second version, which expand one bar (b. 118) in the first version into two, and the retransition following the F major climax at bar 126 (A:125), which is partly recomposed and differently proportioned, although it follows the same harmonic outline and with its curtailed reprise comes to exactly the same number of bars (A:143 = B:144). The result is a movement that only differs in length by one bar (the first version of the movement is 172 bars long, the second 173).

8. The only possible perfect cadential progression to C minor or major in the movement is that in bars 44–6, and as this is already significantly weakened by the stepwise descent in the bass, it is hard even to hear this as genuinely cadential.

9. See Stephen Rodgers and Tyler Osborne: 'Prolongational Closure in the Lieder of Fanny Hensel', *Music Theory Online*, 26/3 (2020), https://mtosmt.org/issues/mto.20.26.3/mto.20.26.3.rodgersosborne .html; Stephen Rodgers, 'Plagal Cadences in Fanny Hensel's Songs', in Rodgers (ed.), *The Songs of Fanny Hensel* (New York: Oxford University Press, 2021), pp. 129–45; and Tyler Osborne, '"You Too May Change": Tonal Pairing of the Tonic and Subdominant in Two Songs by Fanny Hensel', in Rodgers (ed.), *The Songs of Fanny Hensel*, pp. 113–28. As Rodgers argues, in her music Hensel repeatedly 'employed stunningly original strategies to defer, smudge, attenuate, undermine, or altogether avoid expected moments of cadential closure' ('Plagal Cadences in Fanny Hensel's Songs', p. 142).

6

THIRD MOVEMENT

Romanza

This *Romanza*, marked *molto cantabile*, forms the expressive heart of the quartet and effectively plays the role of a lyrical slow movement, even if no specific tempo indication is given. Although quite different in tone from the preceding Allegretto, it shares many of the same compositional features. Most immediately evident is the ambiguity between tonic and subdominant. Hensel's third movement is written with a key signature of two flats. G minor is evidently implied, but the very first harmony heard is a G^7 chord, with raised third and lowered seventh, that clearly functions as V/C minor (see Example 6.1 below). If the preceding Allegretto had left some uncertainty at its end regarding whether C functioned as tonic or as the dominant of F minor, now the same problem is taken one stage further back to insinuate C as tonic at the expense of its own dominant, G. Ironically, too, following a movement in which no perfect cadential progression to C minor was ever clearly present, the next movement opens with a succession of harmonies that would trace just this progression – only that C minor is now no longer the ostensible tonic. In fact no cadence to G minor will actually occur in this movement either.[1] With this opening Hensel is not only taking up the problem left at the end of the Allegretto, but also harking back to one of her Beethovenian models – the opening bars of the 'Harp' Quartet, Op. 74 – which in turn had influenced her brother's quartet Op. 12.[2]

At a larger level, the movement also falls into a three-part layout, with an opening exposition of material (bb. 1–26), an extensive central section that proves markedly developmental and ranges more widely through different tonal areas (bb. 26–65), and a shortened reprise of the opening (bb. 66–82). Although

79

Example 6.1 Hensel, String Quartet, iii, opening, a and b phrases

the opening section navigates its way from an ostensible G minor to an arrival in its relative B flat major in bar 26 and features two distinctive thematic ideas – the opening four-bar unit (a) and a contrasting four-bar idea (b) first heard in bars 8^4–12 – it would be surely stretching matters to claim that the movement is in any unproblematic sense in sonata form. One would be hard pressed to read the opening section as an exposition, and here and more generally the harmonic and thematic structure undermines clear points of formal articulation. Still, such freedom is hardly untypical of Hensel's other sonata-form movements, and the *Romanza* seems to be informed by some of the same underlying principles – a movement from one key to a related one over the course of the opening section, a developmental passage featuring fragmentation and extensive harmonic exploration, a reprise of the opening section with both its thematic ideas returning. Indeed, of all the quartet's four movements this is the one that in some ways comes closest to a sonata design.

Opening Section

Like the Allegretto, the opening section is initially laid out in four-bar units in a manner that suggests quatrain form, a a' b a" (b' . . .). As it progresses, however, the neatness of the design becomes compromised by expansion and harmonic growth, with the result that the return of b in bar 18 is transformed into a more elaborate thematic continuation that seeks to confirm the secondary key to which the section has been moving. Here, however, the music is just as conflicted by tonal ambiguity as the opening bars, and the cadential-like progression into bar 26 is elided with the start of the next section.

Let us start with the opening phrase (*a*, see Example 6.1). It can be divided once more into two halves. Marked by its opening repeated-note melodic figure, the first two bars outline a V^{7}–i–V^{6-5}_{4-3} progression in C minor, though a low G in second violin and viola parts effectively places the entire progression over a dominant pedal. With the opening B natural and F natural, the sense of G minor tonic is destabilised from the start, although the sense of C minor is also weakened by the subordination of its tonic chord to the dominant that starts and ends the two-bar unit. However, the contrasting idea of the following two bars reframes the initial tonal implication by articulating in turn a strong progression to the dominant of G minor. The imperfect cadence in G minor in bar 4 (a half-cadence in North American terminology) is entirely typical at the end of an antecedent phrase and forces us to reinterpret the entire four-bar unit as a half-cadential progression in G minor, whose opening half prolongs the tonic through alternation with the subdominant (I^{7}–iv–I). Still, there seems to be a split between G major/minor and C minor, each of which has been allocated two bars, recalling Hensel's characteristic pairing of tonic and subdominant that Osborne has explained.[3] Moreover, it is worth noting that both keys are articulated primarily through their own dominant at the end of the respective phrases: neither is given as a clear tonic harmony, but at best implied as the absent tonal centre to which their dominants points.

The second half of the consequent-like reiteration of this opening four-bar unit in bars 5–8 is modified to lead to the dominant of B flat, the relative major of the implied G minor tonic, and continues smoothly into a contrasting four-bar phrase (*b*), marked *con espressivo*, that offers a touch of major-mode solace to the melancholic opening theme with its trudging note repetitions, profusion of sigh figures, and dropping augmented fourths.

Nevertheless, it picks up much of its substance from the grace note and paired semiquavers heard on the final beat of bar 1 and continues the descending motion glimpsed in the opening theme (it is largely constructed around the falling tenths in the outer voices) – so much so that its fourth bar essentially retraces the fourth bar of *a*, whose imperfect cadence in G minor easily leads as before to the resumption of the opening material in bar 13. This time it is presented in the cello, though the first violin takes up the former cello line and weaves it into an expressive countermelody, newly emphasising through upward leaps the tritones that had been formed from the compound melody it had played in bar 3. Conversely, the cello's continuation in bar 15 now simplifies the compound melody into a single unbroken line. Once again, the phrase leads to an imperfect cadence in G minor (b. 16), but the sequential extension a fifth lower reverts to the competing tonal centre of C minor, which elides with the return of the *b* phrase.

Expanding on this *b* phrase, the following bars seem at last to break free of the regular alternation of four-bar units and suggest a thematic loosening as part of a cadential approach to C major that might end this opening section. However, the prolonged predominant ii$^6_5$ chord in C major over which the first violin floridly elaborates slips in bar 25 to a dominant seventh of B flat and resolves in the next bar to the tonic. B flat major is the expected secondary key for a G minor movement, though until the penultimate bar of this section Hensel teases the listener with the possibility of a trajectory leading to C major, the parallel of the rival C minor tonic. While the potential cadential motion here is weakened both by the lack of a predominant in this key and the melodic elision with the start of the next section, there is nevertheless a clear point of arrival: bar 26 both completes the first section and initiates the central part of the movement.

It is significant that these preceding bars were the first point in this movement in which the autograph shows the composer had second thoughts. Originally, the passage was two bars shorter, without the prominent movement to the C major ii$^6_5$, and the progression to B flat at the end was less emphatically realised by reaching it through a stepwise thematic filling in the bass in place of the later strong root motion by fifth. Thus, in revising the passage Hensel accentuated the tension between C and B flat by bringing out each more clearly and clarifying the final arrival on the latter as a significant moment of formal articulation.

Development

The following passage of music (bb. 26–65) forms an extensive central developmental section, marked by the fragmentation and juxtaposition of material previously heard and traversing a wide range of keys. For the sake of convenience, it might be divided into two larger parts: first a looser exploratory section that finds its way to the dominant of A flat minor (bb. 26–44), and following this a more directed core, starting with a sequential passage and building up steadily to a sustained climax, which subsides over bars 62–3, leading to a brief retransition in 64–5.

The first section moves quite freely between keys but is underpinned primarily through the bassline, whose relatively circumscribed movement provides a linking thread between otherwise quite unrelated harmonies (a fairly typical procedure for development sections, as likewise for fantasies or introductions). It takes its material initially from the repeated quavers of phrase *a* and the semiquavers that had been heard in the immediately preceding bars, which derive from phrase *b* and its cadential elaboration. However, the latter are now given in a form that omits the most characteristic feature of *b* – its rhythmically varied opening gesture – and become effectively figuration, warranting their labelling as a distinct, albeit derived, figure (*c*). The characteristic form of *b* will not in fact return until the reprise. Much of the section alternates in one-bar intervals between the characteristic rhythmic profiles of *a* and *c*'s semiquavers, though new patterns are also introduced (such as the dotted idea first heard in the cello in bar 30, which gives a martial kick to the quavers of *a*), and from this point the two are increasingly contrapuntally overlaid. Having descended from the opening B♭ through A♭ and G to F♯ and E and hovered between the otherwise unlikely centres of F sharp minor, A flat minor, and E, the first part settles momentarily on the dominant of A flat minor (Hensel reinforces the significance of this stage by adding a bar – the present bar 44 – in the autograph at this point).

The second part of the development proceeds from a threefold sequence given to a two-bar variant of phrase *a*'s opening motive over oscillating semiquavers drawn from *c*, moving up in enharmonic minor thirds A♭m–Bm–Dm (bb. 45–9). However, the third stage breaks down and is overtaken by a fresh two-bar model, which moves back down a major third to B♭. Thereafter the harmonic rhythm accelerates and, through a contracting linear progression in the outer voices, the music closes in around the dominant of G minor, the Neapolitan A♭ in bar 56 moving through a diminished seventh serving as vii^7/V to a cadential 6/4 in bar 58. But rather than resolving here to the tonic, Hensel postpones the real climax to bars 60–1, with their gasping drops of a sixth, and with this slips instead to a 6/4 of C minor. The repeated quavers into which the climax dissipates form a neat motivic link to the return of the opening theme (bb. 63–5), just as the dominant of C minor links to the deceptive opening harmony of the movement.

Once again, the autograph reveals a process of expansion and clarification at this point. The climax and retransition were originally nearly four bars shorter, transiting from the climactic diminished seventh of bar 60 to the reprise (bar 66) in one-and-a-quarter bars. In making this addition, Hensel is reinforcing the half-cadential strength of C minor; just as with the cadential progression at the end of the exposition, the revision serves to clarify the tonal implications of the passage – albeit that the C minor now prepared by its dominant is the duplicitous alternative tonic to G minor.[4]

Reprise

Significant revisions were also made to the final reprise of the opening section. Hensel's first version, preserved on a separate sheet, was eleven bars long in place of the fourteen of the final version.[5] This earlier conception was even more laconic than the final one, in omitting any return of the contrasting *b* phrase and initiating the final tonic pedal much sooner, after only six bars of reprise (see Example 6.2a). Such an early onset of the final tonic is one of the hallmarks of Hensel's prolongational approach to closure and dissolves any significant cadential drive in favour of a slow dispersal of harmonic energy.[6] The revised ending (Example 6.2b) is less drastic but still tonally unsettling and significantly shorter than the opening section, once again dissolving rather than resolving the material first presented. In both versions, the first phrase of *a* returns in an ethereal higher register in the first violin; as with the cello statement in bar 15, the descending continuation phrase in bar 68 is now melodically linked into a conjunct legato line. In the revised version, following the expected half cadence to V/G minor at bar 69, the idea is repeated, but now the entire four-bar phrase prolongs the initial V/C minor (the G in the cello decorated by its sighing upper chromatic neighbour, A♭). Moreover, the expressive leap of a tritone in the melodic line (first outlined in the compound melody of bar 3 and intensified in bars 13–14) is now given three times, before the continuation dissolves into the descending semiquavers that have been heard throughout the movement.

Rather than completing a cadence to C minor at this point, however, the dominant resolves deceptively up to the flattened sixth degree, A♭, and phrase *b* re-emerges. Though we are in the major mode, the manner in which the key has been reached – through an interrupted cadence – imparts a sense of nostalgic impossibility to the melodic reminiscence of this briefly contrasting material, and by the fourth bar of the phrase the music reverts to the dominant of G minor (b. 77). Once more the dominant is interrupted by a deflection towards ♭VI, but here, unlike at the start of the phrase, we are on the dominant of the movement's real tonic, G minor, and the movement to E♭ sets up an even stronger cadential progression in the next two bars, finally leading to a root position G in bar 80. Still, this attempted cadence – the first to the tonic in the entire movement – is softened by the suspensions in the inner voices, suggesting a plagal motion that touches on a C major sonority, and the unexpected introduction of the flattened supertonic degree, A♭, as a suspension in the melodic voice, which once more undercuts the tonic status of the resulting G major chord.

Example 6.2a Hensel, String Quartet, iii, reprise (original version)

Reprise

Example 6.2b Hensel, String Quartet, iii, reprise (revised version)

* New ms page starts here: 3-flat key signature written on all staves, but third flat later crossed through.
Deployment of accidentals inconsistent, but use of cautionary accidentals suggests Hensel assumed A to be flattened.

In revising these final bars, then, Hensel reinforces the sense that G is the movement's overall tonic through articulating a perfect cadential progression to this key that subdues the strong leaning towards C minor – as manifested through its dominant – in the preceding bars, and which had been present through the 'early pedal' of the first version.[7] Yet at the very end, the melodic line undercuts the strong bass progression to G with its Phrygian emphasis on A♭: the B♮s in the final bar's rising arpeggio make G major sound rather like the dominant of C minor once more. At the close of the movement the equivocation between G as tonic and as V/C minor hangs once more delicately balanced: a tonic G has perhaps been granted the upper hand through the strength of the preceding progression in bars 77–80, but it is hard to rid oneself either of the sensation of the final harmony as forming the dominant of C. Perhaps this is the only way to escape the pathos of G minor: the problems of the movement are not resolved so much as suspended on this gossamer thread of ascending G major sonority.

Notes

1. See Angela R. Mace, 'Fanny Hensel, Felix Mendelssohn Bartholdy, and the Formation of the Mendelssohnian Style', PhD diss., Duke University, 2013, pp. 201–2.
2. See also Cornelia Bartsch, *Fanny Hensel, geb. Mendelssohn: Musik als Korrespondenz* (Kassel: Furore 2007), p. 322.
3. Tyler Osborne, '"You Too May Change": Tonal Pairing of the Tonic and Subdominant in Two Songs by Fanny Hensel', in Stephen Rodgers (ed.), *The Songs of Fanny Hensel* (New York: Oxford University Press, 2021), pp. 113–28.
4. It is impossible to know whether the revisions in the manuscript were entered before or after January 1834 and might thus have been made in response to Mendelssohn's criticism. What is intriguing, if they were so, is how individually Hensel appears to interpret her brother's advice: the music becomes less formally diffuse but more pointedly ambiguous.
5. Both versions are written on the recto side of different sheets of manuscript paper. As the shorter version has glue marks on all four corners, corresponding to those visible on the blank verso side of the longer version (which precedes it), and the start of the finale is notated on its own reverse, we can ascertain that this shorter version was

indeed the first written, and the longer alternative page was a later addition, intended as a replacement.

6. See Stephen Rodgers and Tyler Osborne: 'Prolongational Closure in the Lieder of Fanny Hensel', *Music Theory Online*, 26/3 (2020), https://mtosmt.org/issues/mto.20.26.3/mto.20.26.3.rodgersosborne.html.

7. The term 'early pedal', employed by Rodgers and Osborne in 'Prolongational Closure in the Lieder of Fanny Hensel', refers to cases in which a final tonic pedal is introduced before cadential closure has been achieved, and thus undermines the latter (if present). It proves highly relevant to Hensel's first version.

7

FINALE

Allegro molto vivace

Hensel's exhilarating finale initially seems to sweep aside many of the ambiguities and doubts that have run throughout the quartet's previous three movements. Its cheerful opening E flat major dispels the tonal uncertainty of the preceding music, while formally, too, it appears much more straightforward, suggesting for its greater part a sonata-rondo design. Still, as the movement progresses earlier shadows re-emerge, and the formal model becomes distinctly complicated.

Formal Dynamism

Looked at synoptically, the finale can be divided fairly easily into three parts: a sonata-like exposition (bb. 1–57), a central section that combines developmental activity with a new thematic episode (bb. 57^4–176), and a reprise of sorts (bb. 177–251). The sonata-rondo quality is emphasised by the construction of the exposition, which features a cadentially closed opening theme, a clear transition from bar 21, and secondary material in the dominant starting at bar 40. Although this last section is not tonally closed, wandering off in sequence from B flat via C minor to end on D, this open-endedness is not unusual for sonata rondos, and after the briefest of retransitions the return of the opening theme in the tonic serves as a typical refrain initiating the second, developmental section. However, despite its conventional opening, the proportions of this central section dwarfs those of the exposition; the reprise of the opening theme (b. 201) will subsequently occur some bars after the tonal return (which continues with the material introduced in the development section), and as the erstwhile secondary material from the exposition never recurs in the final section the sonata element is ultimately undercut. Instead of this, the reprise continues into new material, and owing to its continual cadential evasions, the entire final part becomes more akin to a culminating closing section than any conventional recapitulation.

As a result, the movement might be considered as being closer to a pure rondo structure than a sonata rondo. This reading would seem to be supported by the disposable nature of the material that alternates with the primary theme on each formal return. Thus, the primary theme acts as a rondo refrain, interspersed each time with new episodic material (the provisional secondary theme at b. 40, the new theme at b. 107 in the central section, the replacement secondary theme at b. 217 in the final section). Still, with a rondo design one would expect a final return of the main theme at the end of the movement, which does not really occur in Hensel's finale. And for its first half the sonata-rondo model – a customary design for a finale, and one typical of her brother's works – is the best fit for the music. In this situation, it might be better to think of the form more dynamically or processually – as it occurs while we experience it – rather than synchronically, appearing all at once on the page or understood backwards only after it is over. The movement starts out as a sonata rondo, but then the expected generic model gets taken over by the new material in the central developmental section, with the result that a structural transformation occurs, the closing stages becoming freer and ultimately *sui generis* in form. Here, one might say, the form becomes shattered from the inside.[1]

This dynamic formal process is allied on a more immediately audible level with the movement's buoyant rhythmic energy and unflagging momentum. Hensel's time signature of 12/16 is unusual, and worthy of comment given that the music clearly moves in two compound groups of three quavers per bar that might otherwise – and more fittingly – have been written as 6/8. Rather than misleadingly suggesting four compound beats of three semiquavers per bar, the notated metre is surely intended to emphasise the semiquaver as the basic unit of pulse in what is otherwise a conventional 6/8: in other words, the 12/16 time signature underlines the rapidity of the music. And apart from the transition material, which appears twice in the first half of the

Example 7.1 (a) Hensel, String Quartet, iv, opening theme; (b) Mendelssohn, Fantasy in F sharp minor, Op. 28, iii, opening theme

movement, semiquavers predominate throughout, being heard almost constantly either in the main voice or as accompanimental filling.

As Todd has suggested, the movement's primary theme, the idea first sketched by Hensel, is a major-mode transformation of the opening theme from the finale of Mendelssohn's Fantasy in F sharp minor, Op. 28 (the *Sonate écossaise*), a work largely complete by 1828 but published in 1834 (see Example 7.1; Mendelssohn's theme is unambiguously notated in 6/8).[2] Besides transposing it from F sharp minor to a brighter E flat major, Hensel elaborates by extending the dominant harmony at the end of the opening four-bar unit from two bars to six. Rather than her brother's impetuous pressing onward at this point, the additional four bars offer a brief opportunity for regrouping and taking a breath; but despite the momentary let-up in rhythmic activity, their insistent repetition of dominant harmony through ever greater leaps in the melodic line coils up energy, providing a springboard for the music to sweep onward again in the phrase's continuation.[3] Similarly, the quavers of the transition passage at bar 21 provide another let-up in the incessant momentum, but by bar 34 semiquavers once again take over, leading without break into the secondary material, where they persist in the viola's inner voice.

Subsequent to the return of this material in bars 86–102, there is semiquaver motion almost every beat up to the very end of this 251-bar movement (in the reprise increasingly manifested through semiquaver tremolo writing).[4]

Such insatiable rhythmic activity is complemented by the harmonic elision over potential formal boundaries as the movement progresses, giving rise to an irresistible sense of dynamic propulsion. Even in the exposition, the transition is elided with the start of the secondary theme, and the latter merges without cadencing into retransitional activity. Moving into the final section, the continuity is even more pronounced: not only is the tonal reprise at bar 177 elided with continuation of the theme of the central episode and made to sound like a continuation of the retransitional standing on the dominant that has started some bars earlier, but the subsequent thematic return of the primary theme (b. 201) also occurs over a falling V_2^4–I^6 progression, as will the new lyrical material at bar 217 that replaces the original secondary theme from the exposition. The upshot is that no real resting point is felt after the PAC in the tonic at the end of the opening theme, way back in bar 21, and it is not until the PAC in bar 239, virtually at the end of the movement, that we experience a conclusive cadential arrival. Even here, the accumulated semiquaver momentum presses on in a final burst of tonic confirmation. The movement's joyful energy has not been untroubled, however.

The Central C Minor Episode and Intermovement Elements across the Quartet

As already alluded to earlier, the central section is preoccupied with a new theme appearing in C minor at bar 107. Up to this point, the music had been proceeding as one might expect for the central section of a sonata rondo, and at first there is nothing unusual about the turn of events: this key – the submediant or relative minor – is perfectly normal for a middle episode. But the sheer scale of the episode is quite unanticipated, and as it continues at ever greater length, the new material seems in danger of taking over the movement. Already preceded by a four-bar run-in, a sizeable sixteen-bar initial statement (formed as a sentential

Example 7.2 Hensel, String Quartet, iv, new C minor theme in central section

phrase type), ending on the dominant, is followed by a modified repetition (starting from the same dominant lead-in, b. 123, now even extended to five bars), which dissolves into yet more dominant preparation and further sequential treatment. All told, the material takes up nearly 100 bars in this 251-bar movement and is primarily responsible for the enormous expansion of the central section to twice the size of the exposition. Lest we should think this an inadvertent feature, the autograph shows Hensel actually increasing the length of this episode by seventeen bars from the original version: the fixation on this material and its overwhelming of the surrounding music is quite deliberate.

This key – C minor – was first hinted at in the exposition. After just eight bars, the transition passage had found its way to the dominant of C minor and remains on this chord for another six bars (bb. 28–34), as if setting up this key as the secondary tonal area.[5] The suggestion is avoided for now, however, and a modulating continuation phrase (bb. 34–9) links directly into secondary material in the more conventional dominant. But when this same material returns in the ostensible development section (whose layout of material corresponds to the order of themes heard in the exposition), the C minor earlier held out as a possibility finally explodes with full force.

The theme at bar 107 (see Example 7.2) is essentially new to the movement, although the distinctive dotted-crotchet/crotchet/quaver opening rhythm and rising contour has been prepared in a new countermelody heard in the viola a few bars earlier (first adumbrated in bb. 68–9 and then taken up in bb. 72–5). Yet in pitch and contour it shares notable similarities with the opening motive from the second-movement scherzo, likewise in C minor and featuring the ascending leap of a sixth from G to E♭ followed by a gap-filling scalic descent back to the starting pitch (compare with Example 5.2). And even the furiously busy semiquaver counterpoint in the lower two voices at this point might remind one of the very similar figuration of the fugal trio in that earlier movement (see Example 5.3). Additionally, the theme's tendency towards the subdominant for the response in bar 112 recalls the subdominant tonal pairing of the quartet's earlier movements, most specifically the tonal equivocation at the end of the scherzo, and the unusual prominence of C minor and F minor in the opening Adagio.

C minor has been prominent in each of the quartet's previous three movements, present in the opening bars of the Adagio as the first sonority heard and as the goal of the first cadence; as the key of its second-movement scherzo; and as the tonal 'twin' of the third movement's ostensible G minor tonic, on whose dominant the preceding movement had seemed to close. So C minor is certainly a tonal area that is marked in the quartet. Moreover, C minor is the twinned tonic of one of Hensel's major sources of inspiration in writing this work, her brother's own E flat quartet, Op. 12, whose finale startlingly begins in C minor and remains there until the coda manages to recover the global tonic E♭. And up to this point, the finale has been curiously straightforward, by Henselian standards, in tonal layout and expression – in marked contrast to the previous three movements, which all had equivocated between keys and cast much stronger shadows.

This feature alerts us to the larger intermovement significance attached to this key area and the question of cyclic links between the quartet's four movements. We touched before on the possibility that the scherzo theme was linked with the opening motive of the first movement, and now in the centre of the finale we have a theme that not only establishes an even closer link with the material of scherzo and trio alike but further brings back their key – one that has been conspicuously present throughout the entire piece. It is worth recalling in this context that Mendelssohn's two early string quartets are among the most thoroughly cyclic works of the nineteenth century, and cyclic tendencies were also present in Beethoven's late works, which served as an inspiration for brother and sister alike. And elsewhere in her instrumental music, Hensel shows a marked propensity to establish inter-movement links: *Das Jahr* and the D minor Piano Trio are two important examples. So what are we to make of these possible links in Hensel's quartet?

Short of literal or near literal recall of material from one movement to another (which is hard to deny as an objective property of the music), the persuasiveness of such purported cyclic connections often becomes more a matter of individual interpretation, and what can convince one person can often leave another sceptical. In this situation, the appeal to authorial intention may seem to offer valuable corroboration: the existence of sketches, for instance, that seem to show the composer deriving themes in one movement from those in another would seem to help establish that these connections were intended, and thus undeniably 'real'. But then, a possible counterargument would run that what emerges intuitively from the creator's unconscious is stronger and less 'mechanical' than what is deliberately constructed (more 'organic' in nineteenth-century terms, the mark of a genius). In which case, how could one demonstrate this is meaningfully present, and not simply wishful thinking? We land back on the role of the perceiver or analyst, and perhaps this is the more important question anyway. Whether or not the creator was aware of these links may seem to provide the strongest authentication for their reality, but this is not always knowable and ultimately is little more than a contingent historical detail. The question becomes less one of verification (is this 'really there' or not?) and more whether it is meaningful to us or not, which depends on one's own interpretative propensities as well as on the extent of the intermovement parallels and known predilections of the composer.

Regarding these intermovement links in Hensel's quartet I remain fairly open. The filling out of the same pitch space in the opening themes of Adagio and scherzo could just be a coincidence, but the salience of C minor over the quartet and the almost overemphatic use of this tonal region in the centre of the finale, with its own doubled motivic parallels to scherzo and trio themes, does seem to constitute a meaningful connection, with potential consequences for understanding the expressive course of the work. Moreover, the finale to her brother's E flat quartet provides a clear precedent for such cyclic allusions, in which the F minor theme from the first movement – the quartet's own disruptive element, and one with more than a passing similarity to Hensel's new theme – is brought back in literal form as an episode that occupies the development section. In so doing, Mendelssohn reveals how the opening theme of the unexpected C minor finale is in fact a close transformation of the earlier theme. Likewise, Hensel appears to vary earlier material in her own C minor development episode but avoids making the link explicit.

Coming to a Close

It is the very insistence of the new theme, the way in which the music appears unable to shake itself free of it, that calls attention to it as a disruptive element, emerging perhaps from a chain of events prior to the finale itself. In other circumstances, a single statement of the sixteen-bar theme (bb. 107–22) would probably have sufficed, but not only is the entire passage repeated in the following bars – already toying with overemphasis – but Hensel even adds another seventeen bars to her first version, which present a third statement of the theme, now a tone higher in D minor. The autograph shows the twenty-one-bar passage from bar 138 to bar 158 added on a separate side of manuscript paper, with indications that the passage replaces what was originally a four-bar link that is crossed out by Hensel. This addition can leave the listener in no doubt of the significance of the new theme, the music becoming almost coercive in its insistence on the idea. On the other hand, D minor itself is less loaded as a key, and it is notable that the four bars that were replaced in the manuscript also passed briefly through this area. In both versions, then, Hensel seems to be fashioning a link back to the movement's home tonic through a rising progression from C minor to E flat, that touches on D minor as a passing harmonic area between the two. In her revision, she simply draws more attention to the intermediary stage by giving it a statement of the theme in its own right, further driving home the quasi-obsessional nature of the material. This rising progression also parallels the end of the exposition – the comparable place in the first formal rotation – which had led from the secondary key of B flat through C minor to D, before returning to E flat for the start of the development section, establishing a neat harmonic parallelism across the two adjacent sections.

The movement's tonic of E flat is reached at bar 177 following a retransitional arrival on its dominant (bb. 167–9) and eight bars of filling, all of which provide reasonable preparation for a formal reprise. Yet what Hensel offers here is not the return of the movement's opening theme, as one would expect in a sonata recapitulation, but instead yet a further statement of the development theme's opening phrase, completing the ascending sequence from C minor through D minor to E flat. The result is that the point of tonal homecoming is desynchronised from the thematic reprise, undermining to this extent the full rhetorical impact of this stage in the form and replacing a sense of clear structural articulation with a more continuous process of return (we saw a similar effect arising from different means in the quartet's second movement). But there is also a sense in which its eventual arrival in E flat resolves the new theme before the formal business of thematic reprise begins, leaving the remainder of the movement free to continue on its own course. This linear process of reconciling the development's C minor theme to the quartet's nominal home key of E flat through bringing it up in sequence to the tonic offers an alternative to Mendelssohn's procedure in the finale of his Op. 12, where the resolution to the home tonic occurs only after the recapitulation, in the coda, via a cycle-of-fifths progression.[6]

The thematic statement at bar 177 is curtailed now from the more extensive form of the idea heard earlier, the opening four bars leading directly to a continuation that advances once more towards the dominant. The ascending progression of diminished-seventh harmonies, underpinned by the strong bass line (moving first by fourth C–F and then in linear fashion G–A♭–A♮ to B♭) and semiquaver tremolo in the upper three parts, effectively reactivates the retransitional tension of the preceding bars, suggesting that the overdue tonic return of the primary theme might in fact form the real goal of the retransition. And return it does, in bar 201; but the bassline in the preceding two bars has dropped from the fifth to the fourth scale degree, supporting a third inversion dominant seventh, and when the theme is finally recapitulated it is over a more unstable tonic first inversion. This $V–V_2^4–I^6$ cadential evasion is hardly uncommon in late eighteenth- and early nineteenth-century music, but more often it is found towards the ends of phrases, suggesting a continuation or especially cadential function. It is, however, one of the most characteristic trademarks of Hensel's brother, used to run over expected larger points of cadential articulation, and indeed this partial resolution of a long dominant pedal to a first-inversion tonic is exactly what happens towards the end of the finale of his earlier Octet, also in E flat major. Just as in Mendelssohn's piece, here the expected sonata-rondo recapitulation becomes overridden by an unquenchable forward momentum. By flowing over first the harmonic reprise – elided thematically with the preceding music and almost immediately edged out by the resumption of retransitional activity – and then the thematic return – harmonically undercut by the 6/3 tonic – any sense of recapitulatory arrival is diffused in favour of a continual, dynamic process, and the reprise becomes transformed into something more akin to a closing section or coda.

The primary theme, in turn, is also left incomplete: the second statement of the eight-bar compound basic idea starting at bar 209 is altered in bar 211 to prolong the dominant, which once again slips down via a $V–V_2^4–I^6$ progression and leads into a new continuation phrase (bar 217). While there is some general similarity with the secondary material from the exposition in its elegantly arching contour, rhythmic profile, and basic motivic constituents, strictly speaking this material has never been heard before. Pressing onwards, the rhythmic momentum maintained through the buoyant semiquaver arpeggios in the second violin, it manages to sound half-familiar and yet fresh at the same time. As it enters over a tonic 6/3 following the initial presentation units of the primary theme, from a form-functional perspective the idea forms a new continuation to the primary theme rather than a thematic entity in its own right. Still, its freshness and élan stand out to the listener, and as this earlier theme does not subsequently recur, there may well be a sense that Hensel is 'writing over' her original secondary material with this new lyrical idea. Indeed, the effect of this theme is perhaps particularly enchanting due to the fact it has not been heard previously. And in continually offering new and ever more appealing material as the movement progresses, Hensel contributes to the joyful sweep of the music, the sense that it just keeps on giving as it drives headlong to the final cadence.

This cadential resolution – expected for over sixty bars by now – is provided at last in bar 239 with an emphatic *fortissimo* PAC to the tonic E flat. But the impetuous semiquavers of the primary theme rush on, on their way surpassing the earlier highpoint of bar 233 (whose c^4 is the culmination of a typical Mendelssohnian cadential climb to $\hat{6}$ also familiar from the Octet) by finally reaching the tonic degree, $e\flat^4$ in the antepenultimate bar.

Notes

1. In other words, just as Mendelssohn demanded. While Mendelssohn doesn't single out the finale for praise, he also appears not to criticise it in his letter. (Given the clear tonality and cadential articulation of the opening, his claim that the music, 'until the finale, is not in any key', must surely mean that it is *with* the finale that the tonal structure first becomes clarified.) Several aspects of Hensel's design, including the formal loosening of an initial sonata rondo structure, in fact parallel the finale of Mendelssohn's own Octet – another work in E flat major.

2. R. Larry Todd, *Fanny Hensel: The Other Mendelssohn* (New York: Oxford University Press, 2010), p. 185.

3. Frances Shi Hui Lee fastens on the same quality, terming the passage a 'dominant propeller' ('Unconventional: Sonata-Form Manipulations in the Multi-Movement Works of Fanny Hensel', DMA diss., Rice University, 2020, p. 80). The effect is invigorating in a fine performance but can fall flat in more staid readings.

4. Exceptions are brief, such as the rhetorical flourishes at the apex of phrases in bars 140–4 (read by Christopher Reynolds as a transposed reference to the BACH cipher (B♭–A–C–B♮); see *Motives for Allusion: Context and Content in Nineteenth-Century Music* (Cambridge, MA: Harvard University Press, 2003), pp. 134–5); the retuning dominant springboard of the opening theme in the reprise, bars 204–6.

5. C is already touched on earlier in the opening theme's response, bars 9–16, which moves to C as V/Fm.

6. As we saw in Chapter 4, however, this same resolution of C minor and F minor to E flat via the cycle of fifths is used by Hensel in the course of her first movement.

8

RESPONDING TO THE QUARTET

Aftermath

Following the exchange with her brother in the winter of 1835, no more is heard about the quartet in Hensel's correspondence, and neither is it ever mentioned in her diary. It appears not to have been played at any of the *Sonntagsmusiken* (Sunday Musicales) she ran at Leipzigerstrasse 3 in these years; nor does she ever seem to have pushed her brother any further for a performance. When she came to start publishing her music in 1846, the quartet was not among the pieces she selected from her by-then-considerable reserve of music in manuscript. Instead, songs – for solo voice, multiple voices, and of the wordless variety for piano – were chosen for those seven works she saw into press (Opp. 1–7).

There is no direct evidence that Hensel was put off from persevering with the genre by her brother's reaction.[1] With no immediate prospects for public performance or publication, the quartet may have served as a compositional challenge, a flexing of creative muscles; her earlier Overture in C major likewise remained a one-off attempt in a new genre. Still, it is easy to believe that Mendelssohn's criticism can only have affected Hensel adversely if at all: her comments on lacking that 'certain principle of life' and what she perceived as an inability to sustain a musical thought beyond the confines of a song suggest a lack of confidence in her own aptitude at the time to progress in larger genres, and the cold shower with which her brother had greeted the quartet obviously did not provide much encouragement in this regard.[2] Instead of large-scale instrumental forms, in the following years Hensel continued her remarkable output of songs and piano pieces. This did not mean such compositions were entirely restricted to a miniature expanse, however. In *Das Jahr*, the grouping of smaller pieces creates a cycle of twelve numbers that runs for around forty-five minutes in total, complete with internal thematic allusions and cross references. And as scholars have noted, even Hensel's individual piano pieces are often quite extensive: a Hensel *Song for Pianoforte* is around twice the length of a typical Mendelssohn *Song without Words*.[3]

The first substantial composition in a large-scale classical instrumental genre would come almost a decade later, following the rejuvenation of the trip to Italy Hensel took with husband and son Sebastian in 1839–40 and the subsequent cyclic experiment of *Das Jahr*. With the Piano Sonata in G minor (1843), Hensel returned to the genre that she had already essayed several times in the 1820s, the last of which being the three-movement sonata fragment that she had reworked into the E flat Quartet. In contrast to that work, generic formal conventions are more apparent now in the G minor Sonata. The first movement calls up the idea of sonata form; the second movement – a haunting conception in B minor – is a scherzo and trio of rather more regular proportions than that of the quartet; while the finale is a good-natured rondo. But closer inspection reveals that Hensel still permits herself quite considerable freedom. Take the first movement. Its thematic layout suggests a fourfold division into exposition, development (b. 45), recapitulation (b. 74), and coda (b. 101), of which each articulates the contrast between two themes presented in the exposition, while this initial section also provides a contrast between the opening tonic and subsequent non-tonic regions. So much may seem unmistakably sonata-like. Yet the two musical parameters – thematic and harmonic – are not congruent. The more lyrical 'secondary theme' is given already in the tonic, G minor, following the close of the periodic primary theme (b. 22), before wandering off through a number of non-tonic keys that never quite settle (a more conventional D minor is initially proposed, but this gives way to E flat minor), eventually eliding with the return of the first theme in B minor which initiates the next (development) section. The logic is still striking: a tonally stable primary theme (whose G minor tonality – in contrast to the opening *Adagio* of the Quartet – could not be more emphatically underscored than by means of the long tonic pedal here) contrasts with the tonally unstable secondary theme. The prominence of E flat and

B minor also suggests the exploration of hexatonic regions around the tonic as an alternative to the more customary dominant minor initially suggested in bar 30 and also prepares the unusual key choice of the second movement. As both the recapitulation and coda statements of the primary theme are given over dominant pedals, no decisive cadential confirmation of the tonic is provided until bar 119, midway through the coda (a technique of cadential deferral also highly characteristic of her brother's sonata forms). Thereafter, the returning secondary theme is liquidated as post-cadential codetta.

In effect, Hensel has deconstructed the constituent elements of sonata form to create a movement working on quite different principles, a more strophic or rotational design, of unusual compactness (the movement is over in about four minutes). This preference for the continual elaboration of a theme is one that is typical of her other, non-sonata-based piano works, in which the music often circles repeatedly back to the main idea, each time presented in varied and elaborated form.[4] And Hensel has not parted ways with her earlier loves either. The *Adagio* third movement looks back both to Beethoven in its recitative-like gestures and to the corresponding movements of her brother's two Piano Sonatas in E and B flat major (1826 and 1827), while there is a strong suggestion of thematic recall of the first movement in its central section. With all four movements run on into each other, the result is a concise and highly continuous work.

And what of that brother? Hensel's solitary string quartet dates from a curious period in Mendelssohn's creative life, an interregnum between his period of youthful precocity and the establishment of his adult career, during which time he came to reassess his compositional direction and ideals. After his own E flat quartet (Op. 12) of 1829, there would be an eight-year hiatus in the production of chamber music, which would finally be broken with the production of the three string quartets published as Op. 44 (1837–8). These works bear out the changing aesthetic precepts and compositional direction sensed in his letter of 1835. All three can be considered major works, but in quite a different way from both his earlier quartets and that of his sister. Unlike those pieces, the Op. 44 quartets are much more restrained and – at least outwardly – classically oriented, establishing an intricate dialogue with generic expectations, outwardly heeding familiar formal patterns, yet offering remarkably inventive manipulation of conventions within this. There is little of the overt formal experimentation of the early works, however, and as a result, they were normally overlooked in the twentieth century in favour of the first two quartets or indeed his final contribution to the genre, the F minor, Op. 80 (1847), written in response to the sudden death of his sister and a few months before his own early death.

The two siblings had gone different ways. Still, in the second movement of Mendelssohn's new E flat quartet, Op. 44 No. 3 – a scurrying, formally remarkable C minor scherzo in 6/8 – we might hear more than an echo of another C minor scherzo in 6/8 time – the second movement of Hensel's own E flat quartet composed three years earlier, Mendelssohn's favourite movement, as he had told her.

A Creative Response: The Piano Trio in D minor, Op. 11 (1847)

Hensel's final chamber work and her most ambitious composition in the classical instrumental forms subsequent to the quartet was written in the last year of her life – the Piano Trio in D minor. It was also in several ways a direct response to her brother's music, again most specifically a work in the same key and the same genre (the Piano Trio in D minor, Op. 49, of 1839). Besides these affinities, the piece could be read as responding constructively to the criticism he had offered her over a decade earlier. The 'form' and tonal plan relate much more closely to generic expectations. Both outer movements, for instance, are in sonata form, while the slow movement is a ternary structure whose subtle combination of themes in the reprise is never in danger of obscuring the overall clarity of design. Themes are more or less where one expects them to be in relation to the tonal structure. Like her brother's music, cadences may often be deferred and sections elided with each other, but their expected location is indicated even when missing, and when they do occur, they are normally in the expected key. And yet the trio is unmistakably the work of no one but Fanny Hensel.

Looking first to the finale, the overall design is much more transparent than Hensel's previous sonata forms, with the themes and larger sections clearly articulated through cadential progressions in generically familiar keys. The exposition moves from an expansive primary theme in D minor (bb. 8–59, itself following a small ternary or quatrain form incorporating a central migration to the relative major for the b section), through a transition setting up a clear medial caesura on V/III (b. 70), to a secondary theme in the expected relative major two bars later. Even the return of primary theme material at the peak of the secondary theme to secure a PAC in F (bb. 91–5) is a consistent feature of her brother's sonata expositions, albeit that Hensel's 6/4 harmony at this point presents the return as more openly climactic. Following four bars of post-cadential liquidation, a development section ensues, which subsequently from bar 119 retraces the same course of events as the exposition.[5] Differences emerge in the recapitulation starting at bar 176, in that drastic truncation is made of the material from the first half of the exposition (which has already been substantially heard in the development section). Only the opening of the primary theme is given, evocatively sounded underneath an ongoing trill high in the piano's treble register, adding a new textural element at this point, before leading directly into the second theme. Still, these procedures are once again characteristic of her brother's sonata practice. More individual is the unexpected cyclic recall of the first movement's secondary theme at the climax of the finale's recapitulated secondary theme, which accomplishes the decisive cadence in the tonic major (bb. 212–24). Replacing what in the exposition had been the return of the finale's primary theme, this explicit intermovement link might also draw attention to the similarity of this material with several other themes across the quartet. And Hensel's movement is further prefaced by a quasi-improvisatory instrumental recitative, which is alluded to again in the recapitulation's truncated transitional bars. While both cyclic processes and recitative gestures are very prominent in her brother's earlier music, his later works rarely manifest them so demonstratively, and here we see Hensel preserving those same expressive impulses that she had picked up from the study of Beethoven's music in the 1820s.

The opening *Allegro molto vivace* similarly shows Hensel engaging closely with the sonata practice of her younger brother, demonstrating her mastery of a design which she had customarily approached with considerable latitude. Not only in thematic ideas but also in formal design, this turbulent D minor movement references several prominent aspects of Felix Mendelssohn's D minor Piano Trio. Most obviously Hensel's opening theme forms an apt sibling to that of her brother's in its opening rise from dominant to tonic and thence to the third scale degree above. But the differences are also noteworthy. Mendelssohn's melody unfolds more unhurriedly, presented first in cello and then taken over by the violin in a continuation phrase; Hensel pitches us already within a seething cauldron of D minor figuration, the melody presented in octaves between violin and cello and further doubled in the piano part. The tone is different: more direct, more immediate, laying out everything from the start in place of her brother's process of gradual intensification. And formally, too, Hensel is for once more direct. The opening theme is spun out into a substantial phrase of thirty bars, whose closing PAC elides with the start of the transition, leading to a possible medial caesura (on a weaker V_5^6/III) at bar 42 that is overridden and strengthened in the following bars. Mendelssohn, in contrast, expands the whole opening section through a process of functional transformation, whereby what had appeared transition at bar 13 becomes retrospectively reinterpreted as the middle section of a much-expanded primary theme group.[6] Here, sister is in fact formally less ambiguous than brother.

A further point of comparison is the use of both major and minor modes of the secondary key in each of the two trios. Presented as a large-scale period, Hensel's secondary theme enters in the expected relative major, F (b. 58), which nevertheless wanders to the dominant A at the end of both antecedent and consequent phrases. The latter is open-ended, however, and leads into a harmonically more animated passage in F minor (b. 96), which finally closes with a PAC in that key in bar 122. Although the effect is more of 'closing material', there has been no cadence preceding it, and indeed the new thematic idea enters over 6/4 harmony. The clear implication is that the new passage forms a continuation of the incomplete previous phrase, with the entire span of music from bar 58 to bar 122 forming in cadential terms a single thematic unit – in form-theory terms, a large-scale sentence with periodic presentation – whose initial major mode falls to the minor in its second half. Mendelssohn, in contrast, gives a secondary theme in the unusual dominant major, A, the key towards which his sister's theme twice gravitates, which is even secured with a PAC in bar 163 (such explicit cadential confirmation is in fact highly unusual in his mature sonata practice).[7] But the ensuing material decays to the more familiar dominant minor, and while it initially strikes the listener as constituting post-cadential, closing rhetoric, it gradually becomes thematic in its own right, suggesting the major-mode expositional close has been premature and secondary theme activity is still ongoing. The subsequent PAC at bar 214 thus closes the reopened secondary-theme zone in A minor. In both trios, then, the apparent promise of major-mode release is thwarted by the turn to the minor form of the secondary key, but whereas Mendelssohn's design, initially appearing so straightforward, necessitates retrospective reinterpretation, Hensel in turn builds an expansive secondary theme that encompasses both modes.

The entire movement suggests a composer fully at ease with the sonata design employed; there is certainly nothing that bears out Hensel's depreciatory remarks of 1835 in which she lamented her inability to sustain ideas in larger forms. An extensive development brings back both primary and secondary themes and (like the G minor Piano Sonata) foregrounds the 'hexatonic' regions of F♯ and B♭ before building up powerfully to the climactic reprise of the opening theme over a tonic 6/4 (another familiar Mendelssohnian feature, and one which Hensel had already employed in the G minor Sonata). The primary theme initially appears to be truncated, concluding after only eighteen bars in place of the original thirty, but its material soon resurfaces in the revised transition passage and leads directly into the second theme, resolved as expected into the tonic (the F♯ to which the opening phrases now lead fashions a link back to this important key in the development). Following a regular reprise of the secondary group and the post-cadential bars from the exposition, the movement concludes with a substantial coda that, initially echoing the start of the development, builds up one final tumultuous wave of D minor energy.

As with the inner movements of her earlier works, the *Andante espressivo* second movement follows a ternary design, the tranquil A major outer sections enclosing a more restless F sharp minor central section (bb. 38–63). Once again, the music in the reprise is altered from how it had been heard first time round, now by Hensel's weaving fragments of the central section within the reprised opening material, as if that music were still ongoing.[8] Yet despite the ever-resourceful elaboration of her melodic material and plasticity of syntax within each section, the intelligibility of the overall design is never obscured – unlike those earlier blurred or dissolving reprises in the 'Easter' Sonata and String Quartet. Perhaps this dual quality is made most explicit in the Allegretto third movement. Entitled 'Lied', this short movement elaborates in typical Henselian fashion on a single melodic idea presented at the outset, which returns throughout in varied forms and instrumental contexts. The song-like theme – the 'Lied' of the title – professes a remarkable affinity to Obadiah's aria 'If with all your hearts ye truly seek me' from Mendelssohn's recent oratorio *Elijah*, which Hensel had heard her brother play to her in December 1846.[9] So much is manifestly Mendelssohnian, and indeed it is hard not to conclude that this overt reference is designed as a tribute to her brother, just as the trio as a whole was intended as a birthday present to their younger sister, Rebecka. But the freedom and suppleness of the thematic treatment is one that had become Hensel's own compositional trademark, and distinguishes her immediately from her famous sibling.

———————

The death of Fanny Hensel, on 14 May 1847, aged only forty-one, was a shock to those around her. Not least for her brother, who himself died less than six months later. Hensel had only recently finished the trio, which had been performed at one of the *Sonntagsmusiken* in the family house on 11 April 1847, and did not live to see the work into print. The piece was eventually published in 1850 by Breitkopf und Härtel in Leipzig, when it was posthumously given the opus number eleven. It is not certain who arranged for the trio's publication, but the generally accepted theory is that it was most likely Felix Mendelssohn who, grief-stricken and perhaps remorseful concerning his own earlier discouragement of his sister's publishing while she was alive, brought the score to his Leipzig publishers in the autumn of 1847, barely a month before his own death.[10] Mendelssohn had visited the family house in Berlin that September and may have selected a number of Hensel's unpublished works to bring back to Leipzig. At any rate, the batch of Hensel's compositions published following her death – alongside the trio, the *Songs for Pianoforte* Op. 8 and vocal songs Opp. 9 and 10 – was issued by Mendelssohn's principal publishers in Leipzig, with whom Hensel, living in Berlin, had not herself worked.[11] And certainly the Trio manifests a more 'proper' – *ordentliche* – approach to instrumental form; while there are numerous touches only Hensel would have been likely to make, the piece shows a much closer rapprochement with her brother's aesthetic precepts. Nevertheless, we should not forget that the piano trio as a genre was generally more accessible and less 'learned' than the string quartet, so generic expectations may also have played a role in this process, as well as the likelihood that Hensel was now writing with publication in mind.[12]

Unlike the E flat String Quartet, of course, the publication of the Piano Trio at least allowed it to enter the public sphere at the time. But despite this, the work seems to have elicited little comment until the reawakening of interest in Hensel's music towards the end of the twentieth century. To this extent, at least, its fate has followed a similar course to that of the string quartet.

Rediscovery and Reception from the 1980s

Left to gather dust by Hensel following its creation, it was 140 years before the string quartet would emerge from obscurity. The modern Hensel renaissance really took off from the 1990s onwards, but already in the 1980s a handful of pioneering scholars were ploughing their lone furrows in the field of Hensel research, and it is during this decade that the quartet resurfaced. It is hard to be entirely sure when it was first publicly performed, but while German scholarship often takes a 1986 Berlin performance by the Hamburg-based Brahms-Quartett to be the world premiere, there is actually a documented performance several years earlier in North America. On 25 March 1982, the Concord Quartet gave a concert in the Metropolitan Museum of Art in New York, which included Hensel's quartet alongside chamber works by Mozart and Dohnányi. The Concords had heard about the existence of the piece from Victoria Sirota, who had recently completed her doctoral thesis on Hensel's music: as there was no published edition of the work at the time, they ordered a microfilm of the autograph from the Staatsbibliothek in East Berlin, and with the help of Sirota constructed a performing score.[13] Four years later, the Brahms-Quartett gave the first German public performance, which effectively marks the beginning of the quartet's revival in that country.[14] The first publication of the parts and score followed in 1988 from Breitkopf und Härtel (albeit, as we saw, in a flawed edition), the same year that saw the first recording issued on LP by a Munich-based ensemble, led by Renate Eggebrecht-Kupsa, which became known as the Fanny Mendelssohn Quartett.[15] Eggebrecht-Kupsa would release a rival edition of the sheet music from Furore the following year, and in 1994 the Fanny Mendelssohn Quartett re-recorded the piece for the label Troubadisc.[16] These efforts were valuable in bringing to listeners this long unknown work, though subsequent recordings probably present a more compelling case for the work. Another interpretation, by the Basel-based Erato Quartet, followed in 1998, but for some years the piece remained largely the preserve of Hensel cognoscenti and those with a particular interest in the rather diverse body of music pigeonholed as being by 'women composers'.[17] Indeed, more attention was probably given to the piece by scholars than by performers and audiences in this period: useful accounts of the quartet were published in the years around the new millennium by Annegret Huber, Renate Hellwig-Unruh, Rainer Cadenbach, and Cornelia Bartsch, though the discussion remained confined to German-language scholarship.

It is not until the second decade of the twenty-first century that performances and recordings of the work really appear to take off.

Within little more than a decade, accounts have been released from the Asasello Quartett, Lafayette String Quartet, Merel Quartet, Quatuor Ebène, Cavaleri Quartet, The Nash Ensemble, and the Takács Quartet.[18] An arrangement for string orchestra has appeared from the Swedish ensemble Musica Vitae, and as we enter the third decade of the third millennium the work is increasingly programmed and a growing presence on concert platforms and the Internet.[19] The rapidly expanding coverage given to music by women composers is of course partly responsible, as is Hensel's intriguing background and the relation to her famous younger brother. Sadly, it is also common to hear and read in Internet and liner notes a fair amount of factual inaccuracy and colourful but entirely made-up detail in the accounts of the work's genesis and Felix Mendelssohn's involvement: an intriguing story is hard not to embellish.[20] But undoubtedly the quartet has become a firmer fixture in Western classical music culture, programmed not just as a curiosity, but because players and audiences are coming to appreciate its remarkably individual qualities, its expressive beauty, vitality, and sheer strength as a piece of music. By now, nearly 180 years after its creation, Hensel's String Quartet seems to have gained a lease of life – the first it has ever been granted.

At a time in which the notion of a musical 'canon' has become a critical liability – exaggerated as to the scale of its existence and simultaneously attacked for what it is purported to include or exclude – it is perhaps difficult and may not even be helpful to argue for Hensel's place within its contested conceptual framework. But it is heartening that after over a century of slumbering and several decades of awakening, Hensel's quartet does seem to have entered the performing repertory of many ensembles in Western Europe and North America, a much more 'useful and solid' marker.

What does the Quartet hold for us now? As I hope the account in this Handbook has shown, it is a compelling work in its own right, a hidden gem in the varied tapestry of nineteenth-century chamber music. Within its twenty-odd minutes, it travels a gamut of moods and emotions, from the wistful tenderness of the searching opening *Adagio*, the caprice of the impetuous scherzo, the expressive pathos of the *Romanza*, to the finale's boundless energy and sheer joy of a sort very few other composers have managed to capture. Startlingly individual in so many respects, it nevertheless documents a fascinating stage in a private reception history, an original response to the most recent and path-breaking works in the medium available to Hensel in the early 1830s – the late quartets of Beethoven and early quartets of Mendelssohn. The quartet opens up a hitherto-silent, untold story in Beethoven reception and the nineteenth century that would become so fixated on this composer. For here, contrasting markedly with the later narrative built around mid-century of the 'shadow of Beethoven' and 'anxiety of influence' – one that still continues to dominate present discussion – we can glimpse a quite unselfconscious creative encounter with Beethoven's final works, not as impossibly distant and unapproachable monuments, but as contemporary musical events and creative stimulus for further elaboration; what impresses most is Hensel's apparent lack of inhibition in engaging with these works and developing her ideas further from this encounter. Her brother, of course, had been doing something similar and no less radical in the later 1820s, but Hensel is building on both and taking their implications further in her own, quite idiosyncratic, direction, at a time when Mendelssohn had largely 'worked through' this stage and emerged with his own distinct compositional voice. Hensel's quartet points to a fascinating and almost unknown avenue of early Beethoven reception, at a time when classical genres and forms could be used and developed in fluid and wonderfully creative ways, quite unlike the picture later ideologically motivated criticism would paint.

There is also, inevitably, a feeling of 'what if?' looking back on this work, Hensel's career, and the course of nineteenth-century musical style. A final, somewhat wistful observation concerns how this work, only quite recently discovered, reveals not only the voices that were all but silenced (of women composers), but of paths not taken by music history, of avenues left unexplored or not fully developed. There are few other nineteenth-century composers of the same compositional level and musical abilities as Hensel. We can never say how Hensel would have developed as a composer had she lived longer and built on her fledgling course as a published figure; would she, for instance, have carried on the more accessible stylistic course that the Piano Trio bears witness to or continued developing the more idiosyncratic formal features of the earlier Piano Sonatas and String Quartet? Still, at least we can be grateful that the inimitable aesthetic world opened up by the latter has finally come to light in our lifetime.

Notes

1. This idea is sometimes proposed (see for instance Peter Schleuning, *Fanny Hensel, geb. Mendelssohn: Musikerin der Romantik* (Cologne: Böhlau, 2007), p. 287); though plausible, the supposition is speculation.
2. For a similar account see Angela R. Mace, 'Fanny Hensel, Felix Mendelssohn Bartholdy, and the Formation of the Mendelssohnian Style', PhD diss., Duke University, 2013, p. 212.
3. See Camilla Cai, 'Fanny Hensel's "Songs for Pianoforte" of 1836–37: Stylistic Interaction with Felix Mendelssohn', *Journal of Musical Research*, 14 (1994), 66–73.
4. On this idea as applied to some of Hensel's other piano pieces, see Samuel Ng, 'Rotation as Metaphor: Fanny Hensel's Formal and Tonal Logic Reconsidered', *Indiana Theory Review*, 29/2 (2011), 31–70, and also Marian Wilson Kimber, 'From the Concert Hall to the Salon: Piano Music of Clara Wieck Schumann and Fanny Mendelssohn Hensel', in R. Larry Todd (ed.), *Nineteenth-Century Piano Music*, 2nd ed. (New York: Routledge, 2003), pp. 316–55 at 335.
5. Viz. P (b. 119), Tr (133), MC (145), S (147). The design is thus 'fully rotational' in James Hepokoski's sense.
6. See the account of Mendelssohn's movement by Janet Schmalfeldt, *In the Process of Becoming: Analytic and Philosophical Perspectives on Form in Early Nineteenth-Century Music* (New York: Oxford University Press, 2011), pp. 164–70.
7. The minor dominant is a fairly conventional goal of a minor-mode sonata exposition and much favoured by Mendelssohn elsewhere, but the dominant major is much less common.
8. A similar effect can be found in the slow movements of both of her brother's cello sonatas (1839 and 1843).
9. Illustrated in R. Larry Todd, *Fanny Hensel: The Other Mendelssohn* (New York: Oxford University Press, 2010), p. 340.
10. See Todd, *Fanny Hensel*, pp. 351–2, Françoise Tillard, *Fanny Mendelssohn*, trans. Camille Naish (Portland, OR: Amadeus Press, 1996), p. 333, Mace, 'Fanny Hensel, Felix Mendelssohn Bartholdy',

pp. 289–90. Marcia Citron, on the other hand, assumes that Fanny's husband, Wilhelm Hensel, may have had a hand in preparing some of these posthumous collections (specifically the Lieder Opp. 9 and 10); see 'The Lieder of Fanny Mendelssohn Hensel', *Musical Quarterly*, 69 (1983), 570–94 at 575. More recently, Stephen Rodgers has argued that the selection of songs in the collection posthumously published as Hensel's Op. 9 shows notable affinities with Mendelssohn's own Op. 9 collection, which Hensel had selected and contributed to, suggesting a reciprocal tribute back from brother to sister and bearing out the view that Mendelssohn was primarily responsible for these works' publication. Rodgers, 'Fanny Hensel's *Sechs Lieder*, Op. 9: A Brother's Elegy', in Benedict Taylor (ed.), *Rethinking Mendelssohn* (New York: Oxford University Press, 2020), pp. 454–73.

11. Hensel's Opp. 1, 2, 3, 6, and 7 were issued by Bote und Bock, Opp. 4 and 5 by Schlesinger, all in Berlin.

12. The Piano Trio is one of the few new works composed following Hensel's decision to publish in 1846. Felix Mendelssohn's own two piano trios also exhibit fewer intricacies and complexities than the string quartets he wrote from the same period.

13. A recording of this first performance is available on YouTube (www .youtube.com/watch?v=aBo_22co7HA). I am grateful to two of the Concord Quartet's members, Andrew Jennings and Norman Fischer, for confirming these details in private correspondence, and to Vicki Sirota, who kindly provided a copy of the programme. The 1982 performance is in fact mentioned by Marcia Citron in *The Letters of Fanny Hensel to Felix Mendelssohn, Collected, Edited and Translated with Introductory Essays and Notes* (Stuyvesant, NY: Pendragon, 1987), p. 155, but is often overlooked by writers.

14. See the review by Albrecht Dümling, 'Im Schatten ihres Bruders. Streichquartette von Fanny Mendelssohn-Hensel und Arnold Schönberg in Berlin', *Neue Zeitschrift für Musik*, 7–8/47 (1986), 71–3.

15. Issued on Frauenmusikvertrieb 68876 (1988), coupled with Elisabeth Lutyens's String Quartet No. 6.

16. Troubadisc TRO-CD 01408 (1994).

17. CPO 999–679-2 (1998), coupled with quartets by Lombardini Sirmen and Meyer.

18. Asasello Quartett, Challenger Records AVI 8553140 (2009), Lafayette String Quartet, CBC MVCD1149 (2010), Merel Quartet, GENUIN Classics, GEN 11204 (2011), Quatuor Ebène, Virgin Classics, 4645462 (2013), Cavaleri Quartet, Champs Hill Records, CHRCD085 (2014), The Nash Ensemble, Hyperion CDA68307 (2020), Takács Quartet, Hyperion CDA68330 (2021). For my part,

I would single out the account by the Quatuor Ebène as being particularly fine, indeed revelatory, and the recent rendition by the Nash Ensemble is also highly accomplished.

19. dB Productions, dBCD191 (2019).

20. A particularly egregious example is the talk surrounding a streamed lockdown performance by the Consone Quartet from LSO St Luke's on 13 November 2020, available on YouTube.

SELECT BIBLIOGRAPHY

Bartsch, Cornelia, 'Fanny Hensels einziges Streichquartett – ein Problemfall? Fanny Hensels Streichquartett zwischen Zuweisungen und Aneignung', in Claudia von Braunmühl (ed.), *Etablierte Wissenschaft und feministische Theorie im Dialog* (Berlin: Berliner Wissenschafts-Verlag, 2003), pp. 135–58.

Bartsch, Cornelia, *Fanny Hensel, geb. Mendelssohn: Musik als Korrespondenz* (Kassel: Furore, 2007).

Borchard, Beatrix and Schwarz-Danuser, Monika (eds.), *Fanny Hensel geb. Mendelssohn Bartholdy: Komponieren zwischen Geselligskeitsideal und romantischer Musikästhetik* (Stuttgart: J. B. Metzler, 1999).

Cadenbach, Rainer, '"Die weichliche Schreibart", "Beethovens letzte Jahre" und "ein gewisses Lebensprinzip": Perspektiven auf Fanny Hensels spätes Streichquartett (1834)', in Beatrix Borchard and Monika Schwarz-Danuser (eds.), *Fanny Hensel geb. Mendelssohn Bartholdy: Komponieren zwischen Geselligskeitsideal und romantischer Musikästhetik* (Stuttgart: J. B. Metzler, 1999), pp. 141–64.

Cai, Camilla, 'Fanny Hensel's "Songs for Pianoforte" of 1836–37: Stylistic Interaction with Felix Mendelssohn', *Journal of Musical Research*, 14 (1994), 66–73.

Head, Matthew, 'Genre, Romanticism and Female Authorship: Fanny Hensel's "Scottish" Sonata in G Minor (1843)', *Nineteenth-Century Music Review*, 4/2 (2007), 67–88.

Hellwig-Unruh, Renate, 'Zur Entstehung von Fanny Hensels Streichquartett in Es-Dur (1829/34)', in Beatrix Borchard and Monika Schwarz-Danuser (eds.), *Fanny Hensel geb. Mendelssohn Bartholdy: Komponieren zwischen Geselligskeitsideal und romantischer Musikästhetik* (Stuttgart: J. B. Metzler, 1999), pp. 121–40.

Helmig, Martina (ed.), *Fanny Hensel, geb. Mendelssohn Bartholdy: Das Werk* (Munich: edition text+kritik, 1997).

Hensel, Fanny, *Tagebücher*, ed. Hans-Günter Klein and Rudolf Elvers (Wiesbaden: Breitkopf & Härtel, 2002).

Hensel, Fanny, *The Letters of Fanny Hensel to Felix Mendelssohn, Collected, Edited and Translated with Introductory Essays and Notes*, ed. and trans. Marcia Citron (Stuyvesant, NY: Pendragon, 1987).

Hensel, Sebastian, *Die Familie Mendelssohn 1729–1847: Nach Briefen und Tagebüchern*, 3 vols. (Berlin: B. Behr, 1879), English translation as *The*

Select Bibliography

Mendelssohn Family (1729–1847): From Letters and Journals, trans. Carl Klingemann [d.J.], 2 vols. (London: Sampson Low, 1882).

Huber, Annegret, 'Das Konzept der Montage als analytische Kategorie: Fanny Hensels Metaphernspiel um "Jugend/Altersschwäsche" in neuem Licht', in *Digitale Festschrift für Beatrix Borchard zum 65. Geburtstag*, 2016. https://mugi .hfmt-hamburg.de/BeatrixBorchard/index.html%3Fp=59.html. Last accessed 9 May 2021.

Huber, Annegret, 'Zerschlagen, zerfließen oder erzeugen? Fanny Hensel und Felix Mendelssohn im Streit um musikalische Formkonzepte nach "Beethovens letzter Zeit"', in Betina Brand and Martina Helmig (eds.), *Maßstab Beethoven? Komponistinnen im Schatten des Geniekults* (Munich: edition text+kritik, 2001), pp. 120–44.

Kimber, Marian Wilson, 'Fanny Hensel's Seasons of Life: Poetic Epigrams, Vignettes, and Meaning in *Das Jahr*', *Journal of Musicological Research*, 27 (2008), 359–95.

Kimber, Marian Wilson, 'From the Concert Hall to the Salon: Piano Music of Clara Wieck Schumann and Fanny Mendelssohn Hensel', in R. Larry Todd (ed.), *Nineteenth-Century Piano Music*, 2nd ed. (New York: Routledge, 2003), pp. 316–55.

Kimber, Marian Wilson, 'The "Suppression" of Fanny Mendelssohn: Rethinking Feminist Biography', *19th-Century Music*, 26/2 (2002), 113–29.

Mace [Christian], Angela R., 'Fanny Hensel, Felix Mendelssohn Bartholdy, and the Formation of the Mendelssohnian Style', PhD diss., Duke University, 2013.

Mace Christian, Angela, 'Sibling Love and the Daemonic: Contradictions in the Relationship between Felix and Fanny Mendelssohn', in Benedict Taylor (ed.), *Rethinking Mendelssohn* (New York: Oxford University Press, 2020), pp. 140–57.

Nubbemeyer, Annette, 'Die Klaviersonaten Fanny Hensels: Analytische Betrachtungen', in Beatrix Borchard and Monika Schwarz-Danuser (eds.), *Fanny Hensel geb. Mendelssohn Bartholdy: Komponieren zwischen Geselligskeitsideal und romantischer Musikästhetik* (Stuttgart: J. B. Metzler, 1999), pp. 90–119.

Osborne, Tyler, '"You Too May Change": Tonal Pairing of the Tonic and Subdominant in Two Songs by Fanny Hensel', in Stephen Rodgers (ed.), *The Songs of Fanny Hensel* (New York: Oxford University Press, 2021), pp. 113–28.

Reich, Nancy B., 'The Power of Class: Fanny Hensel', in R. Larry Todd (ed.), *Mendelssohn and His World* (Princeton: Princeton University Press, 1991), pp. 86–99.

Reynolds, Christopher A., *Motives for Allusion: Context and Content in Nineteenth-Century Music* (Cambridge, MA: Harvard University Press, 2003).

Rodgers, Stephen, 'Fanny Hensel's Schematic Fantasies: or, The Art of Beginning', in Laurel Parsons and Brenda Ravenscroft (eds.), *Analytical*

Select Bibliography

Essays on Music by Women Composers (New York: Oxford University Press, 2018), pp. 151–74.

Rodgers, Stephen, 'Fanny Hensel's *Sechs Lieder*, Op. 9: A Brother's Elegy', in Benedict Taylor (ed.), *Rethinking Mendelssohn* (New York: Oxford University Press, 2020), pp. 454–73.

Rodgers, Stephen (ed.), *The Songs of Fanny Hensel* (New York: Oxford University Press, 2021).

Rodgers, Stephen and Osborne, Tyler, 'Prolongational Closure in the Lieder of Fanny Hensel', *Music Theory Online*, 26/3 (2020), https://mtosmt.org/issues/mto.20.26.3/mto.20.26.3.rodgersosborne.html.

Schmidt, Thomas Christian, *Die ästhetischen Grundlagen der Instrumentalmusik Felix Mendelssohn Bartholdys* (Stuttgart and Weimar: M & P, 1996).

Steinberg, Michael P. (ed.), 'Culture, Gender, and Music: A Forum on the Mendelssohn Family', *Musical Quarterly*, 77 (1993), 648–748.

Sumner Lott, Marie, *The Social Worlds of Nineteenth-Century Chamber Music* (Urbana: University of Illinois Press, 2015).

Taylor, Benedict, *Mendelssohn, Time and Memory: The Romantic Conception of Cyclic Form* (Cambridge: Cambridge University Press, 2011).

Tillard, Françoise, *Fanny Mendelssohn*, trans. Camille Naish (Portland, OR: Amadeus Press, 1996).

Todd, R. Larry, *Fanny Hensel: The Other Mendelssohn* (New York: Oxford University Press, 2010).

Todd, R. Larry, 'On Stylistic Affinities in the Works of Fanny Hensel and Felix Mendelssohn Bartholdy', in John Michael Cooper and Julie D. Prandi (eds.), *The Mendelssohns: Their Music in History* (Oxford: Oxford University Press, 2002), pp. 245–61.

Wollenberg, Susan (ed.), '"Fanny Hensel (née Mendelssohn Bartholdy) and Her Circle": Proceedings of the Bicentenary Conference, Oxford, July 2005', *Nineteenth-Century Music Review*, 4/2 (2007), 3–138.

Scores

Hensel, Fanny, Autograph score of String Quartet in E flat (1834), Staatsbibliothek Berlin, MA Ms 43.

Hensel, Fanny, Autograph score of unfinished Piano Sonata in E flat (1829), Staatsbibliothek Berlin, DB-SB, MA Depos. Lohs 4, 73–6.

Hensel, Fanny, *Streichquartett Es-dur (Kammermusik-Bibliothek 2255)*, ed. Günter Marx (Wiesbaden: Breitkopf und Härtel, 1988).

Hensel-Mendelssohn, Fanny, *Streichquartett Es-Dur (fue 121)*, ed. Renate Eggebrecht-Kupsa (Kassel: Furore, 1989, 2nd rev. ed. 1997).

INDEX

Index

Printed in the United States
by Baker & Taylor Publisher Services